Creative Sound Play for Young Learners

This fun and engaging guide invites you to use sound-making as a collaborative, play-based practice in your early childhood classroom—first to transform tricky transition times and ultimately to support your children's executive functioning development and social-emotional learning. The book offers techniques and ideas for every teacher to reach every child in their classroom, including verbal, nonverbal, and special needs children. Easy to integrate into all standard early years curricula, it focuses on three basic elements of sound: pitch, volume, and duration. The book features an "overview of the school year" calendar and an implementation guide, in addition to a variety of suggested sound-making activities that start out simply and, through the course of the book, expand to engage children's creativity in more dynamic ways. *Creative Sound Play for Young Learners* is key reading for any preschool teacher, leader, or parent.

Hayes Greenfield is a musician, composer, sound artist, and educator, and has been working with young people in all kinds of capacities since the early 90s. Hayes teaches his course Effective Transitions Essentials at the Academy, the National Head Start Association's online professional development teaching portal, and offers a video course with the Global Childhood Academy and from his Creative Sound Play website.

Also Available from Routledge Eye On Education (www.routledge.com/k-12)

Learning Through Movement in the K-6 Classroom: Integrating Theater and Dance to Achieve Educational Equity
Kelly Mancini Becker

Pause, Ponder, and Persist in the Classroom: How Teachers Turn Challenges into Opportunities for Impact
Julie Schmidt Hasson

Your First Year: How to Survive and Thrive as a New Teacher
Todd Whitaker, Madeline Whitaker Good, and Katherine Whitaker

Alphabetics for Emerging Learners: Building Strong Reading Foundations in PreK
Heidi Anne E. Mesmer

Supporting Early Speech-Language Development: Strategies for Ages 0-8
Kimberly Boynton

Creative Sound Play for Young Learners
A Teacher's Guide to Enhancing Transition Times, Classroom Communities, SEL, and Executive Function Skills

Hayes Greenfield

Routledge
Taylor & Francis Group
NEW YORK AND LONDON

Designed cover image: Photo Courtesy of Lenox Hill Neighborhood House

First published 2024
by Routledge
605 Third Avenue, New York, NY 10158

and by Routledge
4 Park Square, Milton Park, Abingdon, Oxon, OX14 4RN

Routledge is an imprint of the Taylor & Francis Group, an informa business

© 2024 Hayes Greenfield

The right of Hayes Greenfield to be identified as author of this work has been asserted in accordance with sections 77 and 78 of the Copyright, Designs and Patents Act 1988.

All rights reserved. No part of this book may be reprinted or reproduced or utilised in any form or by any electronic, mechanical, or other means, now known or hereafter invented, including photocopying and recording, or in any information storage or retrieval system, without permission in writing from the publishers.

Trademark notice: Product or corporate names may be trademarks or registered trademarks, and are used only for identification and explanation without intent to infringe.

British Library Cataloguing-in-Publication Data
A catalogue record for this book is available from the British Library

ISBN: 978-1-032-63697-9 (hbk)
ISBN: 978-1-032-59705-8 (pbk)
ISBN: 978-1-032-63698-6 (ebk)

DOI: 10.4324/9781032636986

Typeset in Palatino
by SPi Technologies India Pvt Ltd (Straive)

To Dorothy and Roy Lichtenstein, whose friendship, generosity and support helped me to create Creative Sound Play.

Contents

Foreword ix
Acknowledgments x
Meet the Author xiv

Introduction: The Quick Start Guide 1

PART A WHY SOUND? 17

1 Dear Teachers 19

2 The Nuts and Bolts of Sound and Silence 22

3 Helping All Children Grow Intellectually, Emotionally, Socially, and Physically by Making Sound and Silence 30

4 Sound-Making Develops Social-Emotional Learning ... 33

5 Enhancing Children's Executive Functions with Creative Sound Play 35

6 Reflection 38

7 Mastering Sound-Making Leads to Agency and Independence 40

8 The Power of Providing Opportunity and Positive Expectation 42

9 The Four C's: Collaboration, Creativity, Compromise, and Community 43

10 Engaging Mindfulness 46

11 Better Lessons with Sound-Making 48

PART B   IMPLEMENTING CREATIVE SOUND PLAY 51

12 Developing Executive Functions Using the
   Five Primary Elements of Sound 53

13 Using Variation and Added Complexity 57

14 The 12 Sound Activities 61

15 Transferring the 12 Sound Activities to Hand
   Percussion Instruments 70

16 Creating Sound Sculptures for Public Performance 73

PART C   CREATIVE SOUND PLAY AND SPECIAL NEEDS 79

17 The History of Creative Sound Play through
   Special Needs 81

**PART D   DAILY AND YEARLY CALENDAR, AND SCHEDULE
           FOR WORKING WITH SOUND 89**

18 Approaching the School Year 91

19 Overview of the School Year 93

20 Year-at-a-Glance by Month 95

21 The Weekly Schedule for Learning the 12 Sound
   Activities 97

   Afterword 153
   Reference Articles Regarding Executive Function 154
   Bibliography 155

Foreword

Self-regulation isn't about children becoming little automatons, slavishly following "the rules" and always being in control. It is about children flexibly expressing behavior in ways that are relevant to the context at hand. It's about being creative. It is about playing freely and with abandon on the playground but being attentive and engaged in the classroom. Creative Sound Play is one of the most thoughtful and direct approaches of which I am aware to help children build self-regulation skills through fun, creative, and engaging activities. The key insight of Creative Sound Play is to make use of something that is tremendously appealing and fun for children—the production of sound—and to embed the production of sound within a set of exercises in which children collaboratively create and perform structured sound compositions. In doing so, children build essential behavioral and cognitive self-regulation skills, including the ability to inhibit impulsive responding, to hold information in mind in working memory, to recognize and create patterns and sequences, and to take the perspective of others in collaborative activities. The fact that Creative Sound Play manages to encapsulate so much within a set of readily implementable, fun, and engaging activities for children is nothing short of amazing.

Clancy Blair, PhD
Professor of Cognitive Psychology, Department
of Applied Psychology, Steinhardt School of Culture,
Education, and Human Development, New York University

Acknowledgments

None of this could be possible without the great support I received from Clancy Blair and Cybele Raver in 2012, my first two mentors in early childhood education. I was listening to NPR one day and there was Clancy being interviewed about Tools of the Mind, an exceptional early childhood program that he had studied and written extensively on. I had been working in Detroit as part of a three-year grant from the PNC Bank Grow Up Great Initiative and had really wanted a developmental neuroscientist to look over what I was doing and evaluate it, so I called him up on the phone. When we finally met a few months later with his colleague and now spouse Cybele Raver at NYU, it was clear that I was onto something very important, and they asked me what I needed to be able to codify the method with "fidelity," and I said a pre-K program where I could work with the teachers and students regularly.

A few weeks later, they introduced me to the Lenox Hill Neighborhood House's amazing Early Childhood Center, where I met with Marian Detelj, its director at the time, and some of her staff. Marian never used a clock and preferred to tell the time of day by just listening to the sounds of the hallways. As you might imagine, I could not have found a more supportive partner.

On my first or second meeting with Warren Scharf, the executive director of the Lenox Hill Neighborhood House, he was giving a tour to some people and came into a classroom where I was working with some of his pre-K teachers. Of course, for me, this was great because it meant I could include them in the sound activity we were working on and then be able to use it to clarify a teaching point I was trying to make to the teachers. And presto, Warren and his tour didn't miss a beat; they jumped right in with all of the spirit, enthusiasm, and love that children have for making sound. They could not have supported my teaching moment more. And as one of the teachers said as they left, "Wow, that was impressive!"

Warren and Marian completely saw the value of my work and made it possible for me to have complete access to their eight classes of pre-K students and teachers for five years to be able to codify Creative Sound Play, write this book, and create and produce the video curriculum that is available from my website.

Then in 2014, once again, I was listening to the radio, and this time, Adele Diamond, another developmental neuroscientist giant, was being interviewed. Adele is probably the smartest person I have ever met, and at the end of her interview, Krista Tippet from *On Being* asked her what she wanted to leave her audience with. Without skipping a beat, Adele said, "There are a lot of people out there without any fancy degrees or job titles doing extremely important work that we need to be listening to." Well, I'm dyslexic and have no college degree, and I said to myself, she's my kind of people and called her up. We spoke on the phone; I told her what I was doing, mentioned Clancy and Cybele, who, of course, she knows, and she agreed to meet with me a month or two later when she would be in New York.

So, about two years later, when I started to write this book, I asked Adele if she would read it, and she agreed. I got an email from her that I didn't understand, so I called her. It was here that she gave me license, freedom, and empowerment. She asked why was I focusing so much on executive functions. Which was totally confusing to me, and I asked in a confused way, "Isn't what I do executive functions?" And as she heard the anxiety creep into my voice, her tone changed, slowed down, and she said very calmly and matter-of-factly, "Hayes, I love what you do, and yes, what you do is executive functions, but why are you limiting yourself to just executive functions when what you do is so much more than executive functions?"

I cannot express the depth of how her words resonated through my whole body and shook me to my core. As a dyslexic kid growing up in the '60s and '70s when no one knew anything about it, the challenges intellectually, emotionally, and socially have been great and quite long-lasting.

So what I love so dearly about these five giants, whom I am forever grateful to, is the humanity Clancy, Cybele, Marian, Warren, and Adele share, and that regardless of my having only a high school diploma, all that mattered to them to want to help, and be of service to me, was the depth of my work, and my commitment to see it through to fruition. Nothing else mattered.

Creative Sound Play is also the summation of all of my work in music as an improviser, jazz musician, composer, sound designer, spatial artist, and educator. There have been many people along this journey who have contributed in varying degrees and capacities and have helped me to define this material and method for working with sound and silence to bring it to fruition. Of course, there is my wife, Eileen; my parents, Howard and Edith; and my sister and brother, Nancy and Jimmy. And this wonderful list of people who have been lights in my life and have supported and taught me: Roy and Dorothy Lichtenstein, Harry Cooper, Ellen Galinsky, Dan Polin, Kathleen Connolly, Kathy Hirsh-Pasek, Jennifer La Bella, Judy Sanchez and all the teachers at the Lenox Hill Neighborhood House Early Childhood Center and their students, Beth Rudolf, Elise Sobol, Steven Antonelli, Marshall Grupp, Stewart Lerman, Bob Frye, Michael Skinner, Tomoji Hirakata, Ikuo Nakamura, Tony Agnello, John Califra, David Gould, Diana Elghanayan, David Leitner, Larry Stead, Mark Trottenberg, Ken Levis, Laurie Coots, Peter Katz, Fred Lichtmacher, Nina d'Alessandro, Dean Johnson, Paul Socolow, Susan Chase, Paul Bennett, Rachel Huchison and the NHSA Academy team, Alan Guttman, Larry Jacobs, Nicole Crochet, and Kalie Riordan.

Many thanks to Fran Bigman whose approach, insight, and sensitivity enabled her to do an excellent job of editing my manuscript. And much gratitude to Alexis O'Brien, Routledge's editor for Early Childhood and Inclusive/Special Education, whom I met at a National Association for the Education of Young Children conference. Without her enthusiasm and encouragement, this book would not have come into being.

Finally, knowing what I do as an educator and my learning challenges, the most fortunate thing that ever happened to me was that my first school years through the third grade were spent at The Randolph School, a very small, progressive school whose philosophy for learning was completely aligned with Loris Malaguzzi and Reggio Emilia, John Dewey, and Lev Vygotsky. Without it, I am sure I would be lost, if not dead. There were no formal tests per se. I was free to learn and let my imagination go and grow at my own pace, and find my core being. That care and approach to school led me to understand that learning and the process of learning is joyful and to always embrace and look for the next challenge. Creative Sound Play is simply an extension of this and supports every child to grow at their own pace and enjoy playing with sound and silence. And through this basic primal human behavior, we can grow in profound personal and collective ways that will help us to listen to each other better and shape our world in more compassionate, responsible, smarter, and successful loving ways.

Hayes Greenfield

Meet the Author

 **Hayes Greenfield** is an award-winning musician, composer, sound artist, and educator who has lived and worked in New York City since the late 1970s. He has released ten critically acclaimed albums under his own name and has performed at festivals, concerts, museums, and clubs around the world.

Greenfield has scored numerous films, including *George Marshall and the American Century*, which won an Emmy for Best Documentary. Other scores include *In Search of Resolution*, *The American Nurse*, the PBS films *America Rebuilds: A Year at Ground Zero*, and *Return to Ground Zero*, as well as documentaries on artists Roy Lichtenstein, Frank Stella, Grace Hartigan, James Rosenquist, Jan Groover, and Milton Glaser; architects Philip Johnson, E. Stewart Williams, William Krisel, and Donald Wexler; and former US Poet Laureate Billy Collins.

Greenfield is the founder of Creative Sound Play, a play-based, pre-K learning system that engages children in making sound and silence (not music) that builds executive functions, social-emotional learning, active listening skills, independence, and mindfulness. His school assembly program, Jazz-A-Ma-Tazz, inspired by his award-winning CD of that name, has reached over 300,000 young people since 1998.

For more info about Creative Sound Play and its video curriculum, please visit www.creativesoundplay.com.

Greenfield proudly endorses Yamaha saxophones, Eventide pedals, and Vandoren reeds and mouthpieces.

Introduction: The Quick Start Guide

Dear friends, teachers, educational coaches and trainers, school administrators, legislators, neuroscientists, developmental psychologists, philosophers, kids, and families—lend me your ears!

I would like to introduce you to Creative Sound Play, an entirely play-based, interconnected, generative, and collaborative learning ecosystem that harnesses one of the most primal, fun, and joyful parts of being human—making sound!

When I walk into a classroom filled with pre-K students, a teacher workshop, or a presentation in a conference hall, the first thing I do is count out loud 1, 2, 3, 4, and keep repeating it but at different volume levels. Medium at first, then a whisper, then loudly, then medium again, and then end on a whisper. Inevitably everyone's active listening skills engage, and they jump in and join me in counting at different levels of volume. This simple activity also engages executive functions (EFs)–inhibitory control, cognitive flexibility, and social-emotional learning (SEL), and is a perfect short transition activity to use with students during transition times! So, let's get started!

I have never met a child, whether verbal, nonverbal, special needs, or even deaf, who didn't absolutely love and adore making sound, whether nonsensical, humorous, scary, or quizzical. Have you? And how glorious and magical sound-making and silence are because playing with sound and silence helps children develop their EF abilities, inhibitory control and self-regulation, working memory, cognitive flexibility, and problem-solving. Creative Sound Play also helps children develop their SEL, creativity, agency and independence, math and science skills, hand-eye coordination, ability to engage in reflection, active listening skills, mindfulness, and self-esteem, not to mention helping teachers manage their classes better.

Sound is communication, language, dialogue, expression, and listening. Silence is the quiet empty space around sound where a sound ends and another begins, a place to pause, take a breath, or emphasize sound through absence. Together, they are art, music, math, science, culture, and history. Sound and silence are a natural part of living.

Just think of all the things that we can do with sound! We can make it high or low in pitch, loud or soft in volume, long or short in duration, and anywhere in between. We can make sound alone or collaborate with others. We can blend all kinds of sounds and timbres together in a myriad of different ways. We can conduct sound by gesture, draw a picture that serves as a road map for how to sound it out, or simply discuss how we want the sounds that we make to overlap and interact with each other as they unfold through time. And none of these activities requires any prelearned or special skills or abilities. All that it takes is the basic human need and desire to make and organize deliberate sounds and silences. And the sheer joy we receive from the experience is the reward.

Surprisingly, until now, simple sound-making has been completely overlooked in early childhood education. This profound, entirely play-based educational tool and resource for teachers reaches and inspires all children. There is little else that I know of that can make children happier, more focused, and better engaged than when they are encouraged to create all types of intentional sounds in all kinds of deliberate ways. As you will see and experience, Creative Sound Play is designed to provide teachers, parents, caregivers, and children with all of the necessary tools with which to comprehensively and deliberately organize and communicate all types and kinds of sounds and silence in playful and inventive ways that help children to learn, grow, and become successful adults able to make positive and imaginative contributions to society.

The Book Road Map

Sound is as ubiquitous as the air we breathe, and there are three very specific areas in which to harness sound-making and silence in early childhood education: transitions times, which are the perfect entry point for learning how to engage students with sound and become the basic building blocks for Creative Sound Play; integrate, transfer, and perform Sound Activities using an assortment of handheld percussion instruments; and end-of-the-year, culminating performances of Sound Sculptures. Each one supports and informs the other, transforming Creative Sound Play into an entirely play-based, generative, interconnected learning ecosystem that seamlessly integrates with all curricula and or subject matter.

The best way to begin working with sound and silence in the very beginning is through transition times, which is why I have created the Creative Sound Play Quick Start Guide. If you choose to begin with the Quick Start Guide, which is highly recommended for the first four months of integrating sound and silence with your students, it is best to simplify sound down to its absolute essence—pitch, volume, and duration. Nothing else matters for the first four months when listening to or making an intentional sound in a specific, deliberate way.

Only after you and your students are playing with sound and silence daily, several times a day, and getting the hang of it, will the other two core Primary Elements of Sound—the texture of sound and how it is performed, either freely or within a recognizable rhythmic beat, pattern, or tempo—come in to play. For a nuts-and-bolts approach to sound, please see Chapter 2, but please know that even if you begin with the Quick Start Guide, the basic concepts you need will all be explained there as well.

I begin with transitions because they provide a daily practice schedule that enables you and your students to focus and work with a set of tried-and-true Sound Activities that solve the challenges of transition times. From my experience of working with countless teachers, though, I have learned that one approach does not fit all. Many prefer a solid linear approach, while others like to jump around. To that end, I hope that you will read through this book in its entirety and see for yourself how comprehensive it is. Sound, silence, and active listening are so much bigger than transition times alone and provide infinite possibilities for quality learning with all curricula that help children develop—intellectually, socially, emotionally, and physically.

Imagine being able to present end-of-the-year performances at which your students can perform Sound Sculptures that include narrative elements, interpretive movement, and children's artworks that serve as road maps for how they want them to be played and sounded out by their fellow students using voices, hands, legs, and a wonderful assortment of hand percussion instruments: drums, hand drums, shakers, cymbals, finger cymbals, triangles, tambourines, wood blocks, guiros, bells, hand bells, cowbells, claves, and maracas.

The Quick Start Guide

    A. Transition Times
    B. Practice Makes Perfect
    C. Let the Magic Begin—Tried-and-True Transition Activities that Work!
- *Quick Focus Warm-Up*
- *Fun with Counting*
- *All Aboard*
- *Sing with Purpose*

Transition Times

I've never met a teacher who couldn't use a great transition activity!

Having spoken with countless early childhood teachers, educational and curriculum coaches, administrators, and developmental neuroscientists, I can honestly say that the general consensus across the board is that pre-K is really, in fact, all about transition times and how children respond, navigate, and learn to interact with them and each other. It is what prepares young children socially, intellectually, and emotionally to be ready for school from kindergarten to grade 12 and beyond.

The best and most efficient way to begin to learn about sound, silence, and implementing Creative Sound Play is during transition times—all those pesky times that are universally challenging for even the most skilled teachers, take up 15% to 20% of a school day, and can determine whether the flow of the day is easy and supportive for quality learning, or anxious, stressful, and unmanageable wasted time.

To understand why Creative Sound Play works so well with transitions, let's simply examine what transition times really are.

- ♦ The sole function of a transition activity is to get the attention of students, focus them, and then be able to seamlessly guide them through a transition from one activity to another.
- ♦ Transitions range in length from 5 seconds to 5 minutes or more, and one type of transition activity doesn't work for all transitions.
- ♦ Transitions happen in all areas of school—the classroom, hallways, cafeteria, gym, and playground.
- ♦ Transitions are repetitive and happen throughout every day, like clockwork.

Now, let's examine how, through the lens of Creative Sound Play, transition times are where the magic begins.

- ♦ All children—whether verbal, nonverbal, or special needs—love to make sound. They don't have to learn anything new or develop any special skills; all they have to do is just be their beautiful, lovable selves.
- ♦ Sound is robust and profoundly flexible, and a sound activity can be as short as 5 seconds or last as long as 5 minutes or more in length and happen in all areas of school.
- ♦ Children love and adore repetition because repetition helps children feel safe and calm.
- ♦ Transitions and repetition—provide a regular built-in time throughout every school day to practice making all kinds of intentional sounds in all kinds of deliberate ways.

- ♦ Children love to learn, love a good challenge, love to build on what they already know, and adore adding complexity to a sound activity through a simple variation.
- ♦ Making sound is entirely play-based and enables children to control their environment, take agency, and be more independent.

Imagine for one moment what it might be like for you to actually look forward to doing transition times—the very notion that on your way to or from school, you might actually be thinking of what kind of transitions you want to work on with your students for that day or week. What a simple way to profoundly change your whole teaching experience, not to mention help you manage your students better.

Practice Makes Perfect for Great Transitions

I am sure we have all heard this phrase, and possibly even to the point where it can be somewhat annoying. But that said, practicing is the purest lesson that I know of that is solely about the process of learning. Being thoughtful about transition times with how you practice sound-making will serve you and your students as you all immediately learn, collaborate, and have endless fun making sound.

I have found that when learning something new, the best way is to simplify it down into its smallest increments or components—and then practice and repeat them until they can be performed with control, confidence, and command. To accomplish this, it is extremely helpful to engage your students by focusing on simple tasks at a quiet, medium, and loud volume, sounding them out as very short sounds, then very long sounds, and finally using different pitches from low to high and back. Sometimes, I even sound it out backward. As you begin to play with sound in these deliberate, varying, and intentional ways, each one of them can serve as a sound transition activity unto themselves.

Here is an example of how you might practice making sound by simply examining something you do regularly when you teach your students how to sound out words. Let's pick a word with three syllables: "Saturday." I imagine you practice this slowly at first, sounding out all three syllables connected and repeating it several times. Then you probably sound out each syllable separately and perhaps put a little silence in between each one—Sat ur day—so that your students can clearly decipher each syllable. Now, from here, let's take it a little further and go back and forth between each syllable connecting them—Satur Satur Satur Satur—and then urday urday urday urday and finally daysat daysat daysat daysat. Then let's repeat the two syllables, but this time putting space in between each one. Sat ur Sat ur Sat ur Sat ur, and then ur day ur day ur day ur day, and day sat day sat day sat day sat. Then, I would do all of it again but backward, reversing the order of the syllables: dayursat. Again, depending on what's going on in your classroom at any given time, each one of these simple variations can serve you and your class as a transition activity.

Now let's introduce pitch and duration into the mix and go back to sounding it out correctly—Saturday—but now making the first two syllables low in pitch with very short durations and with space in between each one Sat ur and making the syllable day sound very long in duration and high in pitch: Sat ur daaaaaaaaaaaaaaay

Now let's add volume and sound out Sat at a medium volume, ur at a loud volume, and day at a quiet volume.

As you provide your students with these types of playful, focused opportunities to make deliberate types of sounds, they will catch on immediately and want to sound out all the days of the week in infinite ways, all the while having great fun developing and enhancing their active listening skills, EF abilities, SEL, mindfulness, phonemic and phonological awareness, and pre-reading literacy. They will take agency, become more independent, and raise their self-esteem.

Your students will love every minute of this learning process, especially when they turn transition times into short, fun learning bursts. Of course, you can now practice any syllable, word, group of words, silly sounds, counting, or the alphabet while focusing simply on integrating pitch, volume, and duration with how you want to challenge your students.

This is the same process for learning and mastering all information regardless of the subject matter, whether in sports or academia. It's just the process of learning through thorough examination of looking at something from all different kinds of ways and angles. The profound beauty of transition times is that they provide regular practice time throughout every school day for you and your students to choose, focus, and perform Sound Activities repeatedly in small increments. This will enable you and your students to easily learn the fundamentals of Creative Sound Play while transforming transitions into spectacular short learning bursts.

Let the Magic Begin—Tried-and-True Transition Activities That Work!
Because the sole purpose of this Quick Start Guide is to get you using sound with your students during transition times immediately, the only Primary Elements of Sound we are going to focus on are pitch, volume, and duration. This way, you can see firsthand how quickly your children get and love it. To do this, let's simplify transitions down to these four specific approaches for making intentional sound in deliberate ways:

- Quick Focus Warm-Up – An excellent welcoming transition activity that inspires students to lead and take agency of and raise their self-esteem
- Fun with Counting – Perfect for short transitions that enable students to control and take agency immediately
- All Aboard – Ideal for those longer, seemingly endless transition activities
- Sing with Purpose – An excellent way to transform children's songs

Quick Focus Warm-Up
This is excellent for always focusing students quickly. It consists of a short 15- to 45-second call and response or a follow-the-leader sound activity done by making and improvising all kinds of fun sounds using voices making silly syllables and/or words; rhyming; hands clapping, patting, and rubbing heads, shoulders, arms, torsos and legs; and stomping feet.

The Quick Focus Warm-Up should be led in the beginning by the teacher and as soon as students begin to show mastery the teacher should switch from leader to facilitator, making sure that all their students get a chance to lead.

What a Quick Focus Warm-Up 15 to 45 Seconds Might Look Like in Practice

Without speaking to your students, begin clapping your hands. Start out slowly, then clap faster and faster. Clap softly and then loudly. Stop for a second or two and begin again. Try to clap fast and keep the volume very soft. Try to clap slowly, but make each clap loud.

Now rub your hands slowly, then faster and faster. Clap once and stop. Stomp a foot. Clap three times and stop. Mix it up between rubbing, clapping, stomping, and patting.

Have fun with this quick warm-up exercise, and change things up and experiment with all kinds of sounds—stomping, patting, vocalizing, calling out silly syllables, crazy sounds, scat singing. Incorporate different levels of volume, etc. *Just have fun and remember to always try and surprise your students with the unexpected.*

Once your students become familiar with the Quick Focus Warm-Up and are ready to follow as soon as they hear you clap, it is necessary that each student have the opportunity throughout the week to be the one to lead this Quick Focus Warm-Up.

Please note that this is just one example to try. My hope is that you will come up with your own versions. I love to make crazy nonsensical and funny silly sounds or syllables first that are short and long in length, high and low in pitch, and loud and quiet in volume, interacting with silence, kind of like bad, funny-sounding scat singing. Then maybe a couple of hand claps, some silence, a foot stomp finished by gently patting all around my body.

So why is this activity so important?

- ♦ This engages your students' active listening skills. By practicing waiting for their turn to respond by making and repeating all kinds of sounds, children develop all of the attributes of EF ability: inhibitory control and self-regulation, working memory, and cognitive flexibility.

- When vocalizing and sounding out all kinds of sounds and silly syllables and rhyming, children develop their phonemic and phonological awareness, which is pre-reading literacy.
- Clapping hands and stomping feet help develop hand-eye coordination.
- For special needs children, patting their arms and legs develops their physical sensory perception.
- Being both good leaders and good responders raises self-esteem.
- Having fun together as a class develops mindfulness and creates more empathy among students.

Eunice, an educational coach to whom I taught Creative Sound Play and who in turn taught it to her teachers, said that their students with language delays were now empowered to be more creative when communicating. Instead of being aggressive and hitting, grabbing, or reaching out to get attention due to difficulty expressing themselves verbally, they were now developing their inhibitory control, working memory, and creativity by using funny sounds and silly syllables. And perhaps this could become a much quicker and gentler leap to developing the ability to use words.

Fun with Counting

Fun with counting is three different intentional approaches to counting numbers: counting with volume, counting with pitch and duration, and counting, clapping, and stomping.

Counting with Volume

Counting with volume is for very short transitions that immediately get your students' attention. This is perfect for when students are spread out in the classroom.

In the very beginning, without any verbal instruction to your class, begin to slowly count out loud at a loud volume, 1, 2, 3, 4, 1, 2, 3, 4, 1, 2, 3, 4, and keep repeating counting from 1 to 4 until everyone has caught on and is counting with you at a loud volume.

As soon as that happens, keep counting, but change your volume to a whisper. Once everyone is counting at a whisper, change your volume to a moderate volume. Once they are counting at a moderate level, change it back to a whisper. Once they are all counting from 1 to 4 at a whisper, the transition is done, and your children are ready for their next activity in the day.

As you continue to count with volume regularly during transition times, your students will catch on quicker and quicker. The more you have fun trying to mess them up, the better. This is all about enhancing your students' active listening skills, self-regulation, cognitive flexibility, and working memory. And don't forget to change up the count from 1 to 4. Count from 1 to 3, or 1 to 5, or 1 to 6, and so on. Count only even numbers and then only odd numbers. Even count backward. And once your students are getting it, have them lead.

Again, once everyone is focused and counting at different volumes, the transition is over, and you are on to your next activity.

Counting with Pitch and Duration

Counting with pitch and duration is the perfect way to count students when lining up. Since counting students happens regularly, adding pitch and duration to the mix makes it so much more fun for children. The more you do this, the more they will do it on their own.

Instead of deliberately using volume as we did earlier, we are now going to deliberately engage pitch and duration when we count.

Slowly count each student who has lined up or is already in line, alternating between a long low sound for the number 1, a short high sound for the number 2, a long low sound for the number 3, a short high sound for 4, a long low sound for the number 5, a short high sound for 6, a long low sound for the number 7, and a short high sound for 8, and so on until you count all of your students.

Of course, as soon as your students are getting this easily, change it up and reverse the way you're counting. Now count 1 as a short high-pitched sound, 2 as a long and low-pitched sound, and so on.

Counting, Clapping, and Stomping

Counting, clapping, and stomping are gaining the ability to count and perform a deliberate, controlled clap, stomp, or both on a given beat.

Without any verbal instruction to your class, begin to count out loud at a moderate volume: 1, 2, 3, 4, 1, 2, 3, 4, 1, 2, 3, 4, etc.

Now that everyone is counting with you 1, 2, 3, 4, 1, 2, 3, 4, etc., at a moderate volume, clap your hands only once every time you say the number 1.

Make sure you keep a moderate to slow, steady tempo. Do this for as long as it takes for everyone to master counting 1, 2, 3, 4, 1, 2, 3, 4, etc., while clapping once every time the number 1 is said and counted out loud. Once everyone is focused on counting and clapping, the transition is done, and it's time to start a new activity.

It's important to note here that not everyone needs to be successfully executing the task at hand, but more importantly trying with intention. It is now when everyone is focused that the transition is over, and it's time to seamlessly guide your students onto another daily activity.

Of course, as soon as this activity is finished and you need a new transition activity, begin where you left off…counting 1, 2, 3, 4, 1, 2, 3, 4 and clapping only on 1. You will see that the more you do this, the more your students will be prepared for some kind of sound-based transition activity and pick up very easily where they left off. As soon as all students are counting and clapping only on the number 1, change it up to clapping only on the number 2. Next, clap only on 3 and then only on 4.

As you and your class progress with counting, clapping, and stomping, feel free to add more claps and stomps on different numbers. Then add vocal sounds like barking, quacking, or mooing on different numbers. Depending on you, your class, and how fast everyone picks this up, feel free to add more complexity. Count backward. Clap loudly on 1, stomp softly on 2, speak loudly on 3, and whisper on 4. Most importantly, have fun with sound, use your imagination, and include your students in deciding what sounds to use and have them lead!

Now that you are comfortable and understand the philosophy behind integrating the basic elements of sound—pitch, volume, and duration—through counting in all kinds of deliberate ways, imagine all the fun you and your students can have integrating Creative Sound Play with any curricula or subject matter you teach every day. All of a sudden, everyone has a new sound dimension to draw from at their fingertips to joyously explore by creatively sounding out the days of the week or the months of the year. What a spectacular way to engage the imagination of your students by sounding out all those lessons, which fortunately now are no longer boring rote memorization but expressive building blocks that inspire and lead to greater learning. One thing to be aware of is that it's best not to stop and overcorrect students when they are not getting it. What's better and more effective is to just slow down the sound activity and keep repeating it. Eventually, they will all be able to perform it. Always keep in mind that the only thing that matters with sound-making is the level of your students' intention in sounding out the sound activity. Not whether they do it perfectly. All that matters is that everyone is having great fun, and they are focused, engaged, and doing their best to apply themselves. Plus, mistakes are wonderful and can be some of the best sounds ever! Believe me!

All Aboard

Creating a Choo Choo Train Sound Sculpture

For longer, more extended transitions, we love to transform a simple, narrative idea into what I call a Sound Sculpture, and in this example, we are going to be an imaginary choo choo train.

Ask your students to line up and pretend that they are a choo choo train. Most importantly, as they are lining up, ask them to make the sound of what a basic choo choo train sounds like:

Cha-gah cha-gah cha-gah cha-gah cha-gah.

Now that you have the basic sound for the choo choo train Sound Sculpture, yell out like a conductor, "All Aboard," and begin the choo choo train.

The more you use it, the more you will want to include simple variations of sound to keep the choo choo train always fresh, fun, and challenging.

Variation 1 – Add another sound to the mix.
- Cha-gah cha-gah cha-gah cha-gah, choooooo choooooo, etc.
- Cha-gah cha-gah cha-gah cha-gah, choooooo choooooo, etc.

Variation 2 – Reverse the two sounds.
- Choooooo choooooo, cha-gah cha-gah cha-gah cha-gah, etc.
- Choooooo choooooo, cha-gah cha-gah cha-gah cha-gah, etc.

Variation 3 – Repeat the cha-gah cha-gah only twice and make the choooooo choooooo shorter so it sounds like this:
- Cha-gah cha-gah choo choo

Variation 4 – Divide your class into two teams and have one team call out.
- Cha-gah cha-gah and the other team respond with
- Choo choo

Variation 5 – Simply have the teams switch the sounds they make.

Variation 6 – Change the order from cha-gah cha-gah choo choo and add a new sound, woo woo, for the whistle.
- Choo choo cha-gah cha-gah wooooo wooooo

Variation 7 – Keep choo choo short, make each syllable of cha-gah a different pitch (alternating low high, low high), and make the whistle long and loud and slide up in pitch.
- Choo choo cha-gah. Cha-gah wooo wooo

Truly, the variations are endless and filled with great fun.

Sing with Purpose

Sing with purpose is a simple way for teachers to take children's songs to a whole new level where children not only sing them but interpret them using pitch, volume, and duration. An immediate way to demonstrate this is by conducting the level of volume—quiet, medium, and loud—by simply raising and lowering one's hand.

To begin, hold your hand high in the air and tell your students that this means to make a loud sound and have them make one.

Now, hold your hand at shoulder height and have them make a sound at a medium volume.

Finally, hold your hand at waist level and say this is for a quiet sound and have them make a quiet sound.

Do this a few times and have lots of fun going between very loud, quiet, medium loud, quiet, very loud, and finally quiet again.

Now, have your students go from loud to medium to quiet but gradually as your arm drops and raises slowly.

In the beginning, play with this when you need a transition activity as well, and have your students lead. Nothing is more profound and immediate than conducting the volume of sound. Make sure that when your students are conducting, they have to include all three levels of volume.

Once everyone is beginning to get the knack of conducting volume, begin to integrate children's songs into the mix: "Twinkle Twinkle Little Star," "The Alphabet Song," "The Muffin Man," "Hush, Little Baby." As your students gain mastery, have all of your students conduct. And make sure that each student conducts all levels of volume.

Of course, this is not just about volume. Pre-K children also love to interpret songs by singing them in either a high or low pitch, and with short or long durations. They just love any kind of challenge where they can twist up something they know, like a children's song, and put their own stamp on it!

Now that you have four tried-and-true flexible Sound Activities at your fingertips to use immediately with your students to navigate transition times successfully, have fun exploring them. Embrace and internalize what resonates and inspires your creativity the most. Come up with your own Sound Activities. Know that as you master and create these basic sound tools, you are providing wonderful opportunities for your students to listen, grow, and make sound in ways that gradually get more complex and celebrate the learning process in all the fun, joyous, and play-based ways they can by simply doing what they love to do most: make sound.

Part A
Why Sound?

1

Dear Teachers

Dear Teachers,

You are my heroes! Over the years, I have had the great privilege to visit countless classrooms and work with teachers of all colors, nationalities, faiths, and genders, and the one constant I have always found is that at your core, you have a calling to teach, love your children and want to serve them to the best of your abilities. With that same spirit, I am writing this book, not for any other reason than to serve you and your children to the best of my abilities.

Given the administrative pressures that you are under to do well, I understand that working with something new may seem a little overwhelming at first. Therefore, my goal is to make Creative Sound Play super easy to grasp and adopt for you and your students as quickly and with as much fun as possible.

I hope Creative Sound Play will be as much about fun and play for you as it will be for your students and that it will inspire you all to embrace a little risk-taking and learn about sound and silence through experimentation. I know all too well that as we grow up, we seem to acquire negative voices in our heads that inhibit us from attempting tasks, activities, and more that we really want to try. I know for me, these limitations are mostly born of my own insecurity and fear of appearing foolish or failing. Please remember that however awkward or self-conscious you may feel making a particular sound, your students will never feel that way. To them, following you in making any kind of sound is the best fun in the world.

But the biggest and most common stumbling block I have found for teachers is that as soon as they hear the word sound, most interpret this to mean music—and how can anyone expect a non-music teacher to teach music? Precisely, and I EMPHATICALLY do not!

Sound is everywhere, and it is ubiquitous. Sound always comes first, before anything we could ever think of calling music, or noise for that matter. Sound is as simple as a bird chirping, hands clapping, a dog barking, cars revving, jackhammers hammering, glass breaking, doors slamming, kittens purring, wind blowing, rain pelting, waves lapping, a refrigerator humming, a horn honking, or a child sounding out a silly syllable. It doesn't matter the type of sound, it's just sound! It can be high or low in pitch, loud or quiet in volume, and short and long in duration. It's all just sound and what we hear first. Then, we decide what it is and what type of category to place it in. The only thing that turns a sound into anything more than a sound is how that sound is deliberately created and organized. Nothing more, nothing less!

So as you can see, Creative Sound Play has absolutely nothing to do with music and is solely and entirely only concerned with creating and organizing different kinds of sounds, textures, and silences. That's it, nothing else. I cannot say this enough. ONLY SOUND! So please relax, take a deep breath, and let go of any self-imposed stress! Slow down, turn off any negative words in your head, and forget any preconceptions you might have about what sound is—let that all go! Creative Sound Play is entirely and only concerned with creating and organizing deliberate types of intentional sound-making, something that everyone is entirely and completely capable of doing easily. Remember, this is NOT about music! This has absolutely NOTHING to do with music and comes BEFORE anything we might call music! This is about just plain old having fun making sound and silence and sharing that beautiful experience with your students.

The most important thing you can do as you read this book is remember the following:

- Sound Making is play-based and Everyone has their own style of making sound and silence, and as long as you and your students strive to be deliberate and intentional regarding the sound you are trying to make, there is absolutely no wrong way of making sound and silence!
- With this in mind, there are only three golden rules about working with sound and silence, which serve as the cornerstones for the entire Creative Sound Play method:
- First, always strive to be aware of making deliberate and intentional types of sound and silence.
- Trust that as long as one is always fully committed to creating a deliberate and intentional sound and silence, the end result doesn't matter.
- And know that the ability to successfully execute and perform a deliberate and intentional sound and silence will always come in time with regular and consistent practice.

Lastly, I understand that all teachers crave short games and exercises that are used for transitions, focus, warm-ups, and cooldowns. Magically, the best, most effective way to learn Creative Sound Play is during all of these short times that happen throughout every day, range anywhere from 5 seconds to 5 minutes in length and happen in classrooms, hallways, cafeterias, gyms, and on the playground. Practice several times a day regularly, and presto—you and your students will be masters in no time.

2

The Nuts and Bolts of Sound and Silence

Understanding the Five Primary Elements of Sound

Here are all of the five Primary Elements of Sound that serve as the foundation and cornerstones of Creative Sound Play and inform everything we do with sound and silence. They are:

1. The pitch of the sound.
2. The volume of the sound.
3. The duration or length of the sound.
4. The texture of the sound.
5. Whether the sound is performed freely or within a recognizable rhythmic beat, pattern, or tempo.

What Does the Pitch of Sound Mean?
The pitch of sound pertains to whether it is high like a whistle or birds chirping or low like the roar of a lion, and anywhere in between.

What Is the Volume of Sound?
The volume of sound is how quiet or loud a sound is. Does it stay at the same level of volume? Does it begin quietly and get louder? Does it start loud and get quieter? Does it do both? Can

your students make controlled, deliberate sounds at three different levels of volume—quiet—medium—loud? Can they make controlled sounds that get both louder and quieter, and in any combination? And can they deliberately make sound that goes from one volume level to another gradually?

What Is the Duration or Length of Sound?
Length means how long the duration of the sound lasts. Is it long and sustained like a race car driver revving a car's engine or short in duration like a single hand clap?

What Does the Texture of Sound Mean?
The texture of sound is the type of sound. For example, when I buy clothes, the first thing I always do is feel the fabric to get a sense of its texture, whether it's soft like silk and cashmere or scratchy like wool or flax. When I hear a knocking sound, I hear if it is the sound of wood on wood, metal on metal, wood on metal, or if it is a hollow or solid type sound, etc. If I hear a voice, is it a whisper or a full voice? Is it raspy, shrill, or smooth? How old does the voice sound? Is it a man's or woman's? Is it a child's voice or one of a teenager? Can I tell the race, ethnicity, or country or part of the country where they are from? All of this constitutes what the texture of the sound is.

Whether the Sound Is Performed Freely or within a Recognizable Rhythmic Beat, Pattern, or Tempo
Does the sound(s) seem to float in space without any specific context much like a butterfly flying here and there or a leaf blowing in the wind, bouncing around with seemingly no real direction, or does the sound(s) play within some kind of noticeable pulse, tempo, pattern or beat like windshield wipers in a car?

Developing Active Listening Skills

To begin to understand how to enhance our active listening skills, here is a very short (30-second to a minute) exercise for you to do right now. Get comfortable, close your eyes, and take this quiet, mindful moment to actively listen, tune in, and identify all of the sounds that surround you.

Listen to how they interact and come and go. Where are they located? Are they in front, behind, above, or to the side(s) of you? Are they high or low in pitch? Loud or quiet? Long or short? Perhaps there's a plane overhead? A car or truck horn outside? A dog barking in the distance? A door squeaking? Someone walking? People talking? Kids playing?

As insignificant as this exercise may seem, being quiet, actively listening, and identifying the sounds of our environment force us to tune in, be present in the moment, mindful, and engage our inhibitory control, self-regulation, and working memory.

Now, do this with your students in your classroom for no more than 30 seconds to a minute. Let your class know that they can hear better when they close their eyes, tune in, and just listen with their ears wide open to all of the magical sounds that surround them.

This is a wonderful way to inspire mindfulness and, when it's over, stimulate intellectual curiosity and discussion by identifying all the types of sounds they've heard, which directions they came from, and what kinds of pitches, volumes, textures, and durations they noticed. Were there any sounds that kept a constant beat or tempo?

Do this same mindful listening activity every day and at different times of the day. Do it in all the areas of your school—the classroom, hallways, stairways, cafeteria, gym, and outside on the playground. Listen and discuss how each location has its own set of sounds to listen for, hear, and identify. Share with your students that each location—classroom, hallway, stairway, gym, cafeteria, and playground—all sound different. In the movie business, they refer to these different types of location sounds as room tones, and every location has its own individual type of sound or room tone. For example, the classroom has probably no or very little reverberation or echo, making it easier to understand when someone is speaking, as opposed to a gym where the sound is usually very boomy and loud, where sounds last for a few seconds and fade out over time, making it hard to distinguish between words.

And with teachers, as your active listening skills deepen and become a natural part of your teaching toolkit, you will gain a greater ability to respond to your students in more flexible, comprehensive, and less punitive ways that inspire greater mindfulness and SEL for your students. For example, Jennifer, a teacher and floater (someone who works in all classrooms), shared that one day, a student was completing a jigsaw puzzle and got frustrated because he couldn't figure out how the last piece fit in. Instead of being calm, he got more and more frustrated until he started to slam the last piece onto the puzzle. Now, because of her enhanced sound and active listening skills, instead of being punitive and telling her student not to slam the puzzle piece, she was able to respond to him nonverbally through sound and slapped the table, matching his volume. This immediately got his attention, and as their dialogue of slapping the table progressed, she got softer, and he got softer. Then, another teacher joined in by making a clap, which reinforced the magic of sound. This nonverbal sound oriented interaction enabled him to have fun, redirect his energy, and turn a frustrating situation into a play-based one where he could simply self-regulate his own emotions, calm down, and figure out how to put the puzzle piece in correctly.

Something I always do when a child is very loud is tell them that I like their sound, and I wonder if they can make that same sound quietly, then at a medium volume, again very loud, and finally quietly again. After all, every child loves a good challenge.

These two very specific examples illustrate how a situation that usually may end in some kind of punitive experience for a child can now be transformed into a wonderful opportunity for teachers and children to make controlled and deliberate sound together. Whether through spontaneous nonverbal action, like Jennifer did, or verbal instruction, as I did, both experiences provide children with concrete ways to engage with making sound at different volume levels. This not only helps to develop greater mastery of sound-making in general but immediately enables children to interact, internalize, reflect, understand, and grasp that how and what they do matters, and they are part of a larger community.

Key Aspects of Sound and Silence

- Sound is playful.
- Sound is ubiquitous.
- Sound and silence enhance children's SEL and EF abilities.
- Sound requires no special knowledge, resources, language skills, or training for teachers or children.
- Creating deliberate sound(s) and silence(s) requires focus, intention, effort, concentration, collaboration, active listening skills, and hand-eye coordination.
- Sounds and silences can be made in large groups, small groups, and alone.
- Sound and silence are collaborative in nature, and children experience opportunities to be good leaders, as well as good responders, raising everyone's self-esteem.
- Sounds tell stories, communicate feelings, and describe environments.
- Sounds and silences enhance children's awareness and sharpen and improve their perceptual abilities.
- Sounds and silences provide a natural platform to weave in many levels of creative complexity.
- Sounds and silences can easily be incorporated into traditional educational curricula.
- Sounds and silences are play-based and give children joy.
- Sounds and silences inspire children to move, play, and make "noise."
- Organizing sounds and silences provides opportunities for children to publicly perform sound compositions called Sound Sculptures.

A Word on Silence

- Playing silence is a deliberate, intentional action that creates space in between sounds. It allows for air and is a place to pause and breathe.
- Silence is as important as sound, if not more so, and defines the space in which sound is heard.

- Playing silence helps to develop inhibitory control and self-regulation.
- For children, playing silence is as much fun as playing sound. For them, it's all a part of the same joyful, creative experience. And depending on the intention of the silence, children love playing a loud silence as much as a soft silence.
- Silence builds emotional tension in anticipation of the next sound.
- Silence provides release and relief from previous sound.
- When playing silence is coupled with closing one's eyes, breathing slowly with control, and active listening to the natural sounds in our environments, we become more mindful, present in the moment, calm, listen more acutely, and hear more.
- And when silence becomes deafening, it's time to make sound.

The Seven Basic Principles and Philosophy

Creative Sound Play is founded upon seven major principles that drive its underlying teaching philosophy. It applies equally to both students and teachers.

- Working with sound is always about play, and, most importantly, it should be fun for everyone—students and teachers alike!
- Remember, there is no wrong way of working with sound and silence as long as the intention is pure and deliberate. Everyone has their own style, which always needs to be encouraged, celebrated, and reinforced.
- Success is only determined by the level of depth of the intention to execute a given task, not by innate ability or by the level of correctness with which the task is performed.
- Make sound-making a creative experience for yourself. Take risks and try new ways to do things with your

students. Be thorough, take your time, and accept that all may not work the first or second time you try or even reach the level of your own expectations. Always be open-minded and examine through careful, loving observation as to why something didn't work as well as you would have hoped. As you gain mastery of sound-making, never be afraid to revisit something down the line that may not have worked earlier due to your own inexperience. It's amazing how fast we become proficient with implementing sound-making and are able to engage with it in more effective and inventive ways.

- The role of the teacher is to first lead, demonstrate, and then guide each of their students to experience and participate as both a leader and ensemble player.
- An action, task, exercise, or activity that is simple becomes the perfect exercise in which to use variation in order to expand the components and create complexity.
- An action, task, exercise, or activity that is difficult to execute becomes the perfect exercise upon which to focus, slow down, dissect, and simplify the components.

The Five Teaching Protocols

- Call and Response—the basic form of any communication. One person leads, and one person or group responds or follows.
- Looping—similar to call and response, but the leader keeps repeating the phrase or activity over and over again without stopping until everyone has joined in and is performing the activity in sync with the leader.
- Repetition and Focus—(for example) pick one sound activity—counting, clapping, and stomping—and work with it exclusively and include all kinds of variations of it. Do this for however long it takes, whether a day or two weeks for everyone—teachers and students alike—to master and lead the class before introducing another, entirely new sound activity into the mix.

- Slow It Down—mastery only comes from the ability to deliberately perform a task with control, confidence, and command. When creating sound in a variety of ways, it is essential to slow the tempo of the activity down to a tempo and pace where everyone can create it comfortably and with control before speeding it up.
- The Use of Variation—this is performing the same task in a variety of ways to enhance technical ability and gain greater mastery (see Chapter 13 Using Variation and Added Complexity). As neuroscientist Adele Diamond has said, "Sound is ever-present, and it's simple. ... It's so rich. ... So out of something so simple, there's a world of possibilities...infinite possibilities."

3

Helping All Children Grow Intellectually, Emotionally, Socially, and Physically by Making Sound and Silence

Making deliberate and intentional sound and silence teaches the whole child and reinforces a child's love of learning and of being challenged. This practice motivates them to achieve more at school. This simple action transforms into a profound, robust array of tools and resources that help children grow intellectually, emotionally, physically, and socially:

- ♦ When creating deliberate and intentional sound and silence, children are engaged in active listening and become more aware of the world around them. They listen with greater focus and intent and become more able to perceive how their own sound interacts with that of others. This reinforces their sense that what they do matters, how they make sound impacts their community, that they are a part of a larger world, and that they can make a difference.
- ♦ Making deliberate and intentional sound and silence of different pitches, volumes, lengths, and textures is

a challenging and playful way to focus mental concentration. And when including using their bodies—hands, arms, legs, and feet—they enhance hand-eye coordination.

- Making sound and silence is a flexible activity that easily integrates with all educational curricula, whether students are speaking, telling stories, and sounding out numbers, letters, syllables, days of the week, months of the year, words, animal sounds, sentences, and much more. Employing deliberate, intentional ways to create sound transforms the mundane process of memorization into quality, playful, concrete learning for teachers and children alike.
- Active listening and being aware of sound and silence is also just using common sense. It is being present in the moment. It is listening and paying attention to how we communicate when we are excited, calm, happy, and sad, and it provides the space and silence for one to be heard and listened to. Active listening can be the first line of defense for sounds that are out of sight and might pose a threat: a speeding car, a motorcycle, someone yelling, people fighting, an emergency vehicle. Or for those in the home: tone and texture of voice, quiet and stern, yelling and out of control, banging, slamming doors, etc.
- Making sound and silence is a playful activity for the entire class as one large group, or a combination of smaller groups, or individual students, or in any combination of these. With everyone sharing a common goal, the class transforms into a cohesive working ensemble. Waiting one's turn and having patience becomes everyday behavior.
- Making sound and silence provides the platform for adding variation and complexity by making all kinds of additional, deliberate, intentional sounds, silences, and textures. These layers of complexity challenge, inspire, and give children greater control, ability, and mastery of sound creation, resulting in feelings of personal achievement, accomplishment, success, and self-esteem.

- This wealth of new tools enables children to express themselves more thoroughly, deliberately, and intentionally. As they grow with sound and silence, children naturally become more reflective, eager to lead, independent, and create their own Sound Sculptures, as well as support one another and perform as fellow ensemble players.

4

Sound-Making Develops Social-Emotional Learning

The elegance of sound-making is that, at its core, it is collaborative in nature and inspires students to actively listen to each other. This fundamental aspect helps children understand that what they do matters and affects the class as a whole. They learn and experience that the better listeners we are, the more we are able to communicate with each other, and the more we listen, the more we are able to be heard. This helps us to be kinder and more empathetic with each other, enabling greater personal and social awareness of how to trust, negotiate, and resolve conflicts more easily and more amicably.

Because sound-making is so primal, immediate, and fun to do with peers, it enables all children—whether verbal, non-verbal, or special needs—to grow and develop their social-emotional learning in all kinds of comprehensive ways that inspire them to feel safe, happy, and trusting. This level of security and knowledge of what to expect helps children be present and helps them inhibit their impulsive responding and grow past challenging behaviors.

This entirely play-based, collaborative platform provides every child with the opportunity to participate both as a leader and a responder, and celebrates that everyone has their own style and way of making sound. This approach supports, inspires, and enables all children from the shyest to the most gregarious to stand in front of their peers and lead them in sound-making, as well as stand next to their peers as fellow responders engaging as an attentive ensemble.

There is nothing that transforms a class into a seamless ensemble more than the shared play-based experience and process of making deliberate and intentional sound together, messing it up, laughing together, repeating it, slowing it down, speeding it up, focusing in on it, mastering it, messing it up some more and laughing, varying it up a little bit with added complexity, and mastering it again.

5

Enhancing Children's Executive Functions with Creative Sound Play

In the last three decades, developmental cognitive neuroscience research has clearly established that children who exhibit enhanced EF skills are more school-ready and more likely to enjoy learning, to do better in school, and to go on to finish college, and that EF skills are more effective in predicting a child's outcomes in school than an intelligence quotient (IQ). Finally, unlike IQ, which we are born with and cannot be changed, EF skills can be developed and enhanced.

EF is a broad term that encompasses three core attributes:

I. Inhibitory Control, Attention, and Self-Regulation
    The ability to do the following:
    ♦ Be present in the moment
    ♦ Resist first impulses
    ♦ Think before you speak
    ♦ Try something for the first time or try to change how you do something
    ♦ Not go on automatic but concentrate on what you are doing

- Develop the discipline to follow through with an activity that may be boring or that you are tired of and do not want to do anymore
- Develop the ability to focus and be engaged without being easily distracted

- *With Creative Sound Play, children gain inhibitory control, attention, and self-regulation by doing the following*:
  - Waiting for their turn to create sounds and silence
  - Actively listening before making sound
  - Performing deliberate types of sounds and silences as routines
  - Creating sounds with specific pitches, levels of volume, types of accents and deliberate textures
  - Being present and tuning in to what is happening in the moment
  - Performing intentional sounds and silences within a repetitive rhythmic pattern
  - Being able to create sound in the same deliberate and intentional way using either voices, arms, hands, legs and feet as sound makers, or hand percussion instruments

II. Cognitive Flexibility and Creativity
  The ability to do the following:
  - Problem-solve
  - Be creative and think outside the box, improvise, and come up with new, inventive ideas
  - Be flexible and be able to take advantage of serendipity and change from one direction to another at the spur of the moment

- *With Creative Sound Play, children develop flexibility and enhance creativity by doing the following*:
  - Improvising with all types of sounds
  - Creating infinite possibilities to engage Pitch, Volume, Duration, Texture, and Accents whether the sound is performed freely or within a recognizable rhythmic beat, pattern, or tempo

- Performing one sound activity through different types of variations
- Creating Sound Sculptures that can be performed publicly
- Listening, improvising, and creating dialogue through only the use of sounds and silences, no words
- Interpreting art through creating sound

III. Working Memory
   The ability to do the following:
   - Hold all of the possibilities in mind and retain information that relates to an earlier subject while also considering something that is in the present or future
   - Being able to follow directions and maintain focus

- *With Creative Sound Play, children enhance their working memory by holding in mind the steps of a routine that include the following*:
   - Being able to follow directions and maintain focus
   - Manage time by creating sound and silences with different lengths and durations
   - Performing one sound activity through different types of variations
   - Creating sounds of similar and/or different textures, volumes, and accents, that are performed freely or within a rhythmic pattern
   - Transferring Sound Activities to hand percussion instruments
   - Performing Sound Sculptures publicly

6

Reflection

Sound helps and inspires children to examine and reflect in many ways. It can be as simple as when they are following the leader in making a sound, are they following the directions correctly, or do they have to adjust somehow to match the task at hand and the intentional type of sound the leader is making? Are they too loud or too soft? Are they blending in with their fellow ensemble members and peers well?

When they are listening to and discussing sound, how does it make them feel? Do the sounds of chirping birds out of the window, the waves on a beach, a dog barking off in the distance, or kids playing in a playground calm and soothe them? Does the roar of a charging fire truck with its siren blaring barreling down the street warning of danger make them feel scared or reassured that rescue workers are on their way? When they hear the sound of wind or teeth chattering, do they think of cold, or do they think of summer and heat when they hear the sound of bacon sizzling away in a frying pan? What does love or positive encouragement sound like? What kinds of sounds invigorate them?

And how do they feel when they have the opportunity to lead sound-making. Jennifer (a floater and teacher who works with all classes) noted that one of her 3-year-old students was so quiet and shy she thought she would need an evaluation until Creative Sound Play provided her the platform to engage the child with sound. As her student began leading and conducting her peers through gesture and making all kinds of fun crazy sounds, she became more and more animated, focused, and engaged, and as the little girl started to raise her hands in bigger and wider gestures, her fellow peers got louder and louder because they wanted to give her everything she wanted, crescendoing finally into a beautiful madness of sound, empowering this little girl to throw her arms up in the air with complete abandon, break through her shyness, and totally blossom. From that day forward, that little girl was coaching and empowering other shy children on how to break through their comfort zones and transcend their shyness. Who knows where this new, stronger self will take her?

7

Mastering Sound-Making Leads to Agency and Independence

Because sound-making is such a fun primal activity and one that every child loves and adores doing, it's easy to inspire children to master making intentional sounds in specific and deliberate ways. As children gain mastery and control of sound-making in general, children naturally want to take agency and lead, which inspires their independence.

Of course, like everything worthwhile, practice makes perfect, and the best way for children to learn and develop facility with thoughtful sound-making is through experiencing regular, daily opportunities to play and interact with sound. This can happen perfectly through transition times, which occur throughout the school day almost like clockwork, and provide natural, built-in opportunities for children to make and practice all kinds of intentional sound in specific deliberate ways (see the Quick Start Guide).

The key, in the very beginning, is to choose and pick one or two ways you can make an intentional sound in a specific, deliberate way that resonates with you. Now, engage your students with only these few (one, two, or three) very specific sound-making activities and repeat and use them for all of your transition activities throughout the day for a few (or several) days or until you see that all of your students are grasping and engaging with them.

Know that as your students are empowered to have fun with these play-based, sound-making transition activities, they will all naturally become more and more comfortable and eager to take agency and lead them. No longer will transition times be challenging for teachers and students alike.

8

The Power of Providing Opportunity and Positive Expectation

Until now, sound and silence as an educational tool have been completely overlooked. Could it be because sound is ubiquitous and everywhere, like the air we breathe, free-spirited, unorganized, and seemingly unimportant? Or possibly because sound is with us 24 hours a day, even when we are "sound" asleep? Maybe because as we get older, we develop valuable skills to turn it off and tune out sound so as to preserve our energy and limit the amount of stimulus to our senses. Or maybe because it's free, and we just take it for granted.

Regardless of why, sound and silence provide teachers with tremendous tools and opportunities that teach every child—whether verbal, nonverbal, or special needs—that what they do matters! Sound is immediate; it's physical because it takes up space, and it is like magic for children. Children don't have to learn anything new or develop any special skills; all they have to do is just be their beautiful, lovable selves. Plus, the more we actively listen and tune in to the sounds in our environment, the better we are able to teach, interact, communicate, learn, and grow intellectually, socially, emotionally, and physically—an excellent and accessible way of providing children with the opportunity to be reflective, share, and discuss all the sounds they've heard or made.

9

The Four C's

Collaboration, Creativity, Compromise, and Community

- The desire of diverse people to play, listen, and interact with each other supportively
- Inspiring each student to share their ideas with each other freely and supportively
- Choosing together which ideas to use at any given moment
- Playing together successfully as one ensemble that inspires individual respect, empathy, support, and diversity in pursuit of a shared common goal

Because sound-making is collaborative in nature, it inspires children's creativity in a wonderful world of infinite possibilities that are as simple as the following:

- Two or more children listening to each other clapping
- Two or more children engaging in a call-and-response type dialogue using all kinds of sounds, verbal, nonverbal, silly syllables, claps, rubs, foot stomps

- Children trying to outdo each other with how they make an intentional sound in a deliberate way—counting, clapping, and using all kinds of sounds
- Two or more children engaging in a free, unstructured dialogue using all kinds of sounds
- One child leading and conducting their peers as an ensemble making all kinds of sounds

Kristin, an educational coach to whom I was teaching Creative Sound Play, shared a story with me from her pre-K teachers about children taking turns spinning around in the only cup on the playground.

At first, there were only two little boys, one in the cup spinning and the other counting from 1 to 10. Of course, the boy counting was counting as fast as he could so he could get in the cup, causing the boy in the cup to get upset because he didn't have enough time. So the teacher, who loves working with Creative Sound Play, asked the boy, "How can you change the way you're counting?" At this point, he engaged his EF abilities—inhibitory control, working memory, and creativity—and began counting slowly using pitch and duration. A long low sound for the number 1, a short high sound for the number 2, a long low sound for the number 3, and high short sound for 4, and so on up to 10. I know his teacher had been doing something similar in class that week but with the days of the week and sounding them out by syllables. The first syllable(s) for every day—"Mon," "Tues," "Wednes," "Thurs," "Fri," "Satur," and "Sun"—were all low in pitch and long in duration, and each syllable for "day" was high in pitch and short in duration.

Clearly, by engaging his working memory, he had an intentional way to sound out and count numbers in a deliberate way using pitch and duration, which simply helped him manage the time more appropriately so that both boys were happier playing together. Then when they switched places, the little boy who was in the cup started to count but wanted to count differently and came up with his own way of counting. This engaged his creativity, working memory, and self-regulation. "And before you knew it...there were six boys taking turns counting, managing their time, and all counting in their own way."

I could not dream up a better story for how making play-based sound can help children collaborate with each other more, use their creativity more, compromise more, and be more aware of their community. And in the end, it sounds like all those kids had forgotten about the cup and were having much more fun just counting and doing math while trying to outdo each other in the most inspired, competitive, and loving way.

10

Engaging Mindfulness

Probably the most important activity for inspiring mindfulness is when children have the opportunity to actively listen to all kinds of sounds and silences, the opportunity to make all kinds of sounds and silences, and then the opportunity to discuss and share all that they've made and heard. When children do this on a daily basis, they can easily see and internalize for themselves the profound impact sound can have on their ability to focus, concentrate, and learn.

Teachers who work with Creative Sound Play tell me that when their classrooms get too loud, their students actually ask for the class to quiet down. Imagine 3-year-olds coming into a classroom and being mindful enough to ask their fellow students to quiet down. In Sarah's class, students took turns being the "conductor," whose job it was to oversee the class, and when it got too loud, they would gesture with their hands to quiet down or to stop talking when the teacher was speaking.

Having fun listening, playing, and interacting with pure sound helps the internal workings of a class transform into a smooth, easygoing ensemble where children are more empathetic with each other and look out for and take care of each other. I have been in countless classrooms and asked children, "Who hasn't led yet," and those who raised their arms pointed to or said which child hasn't had the opportunity to lead yet.

I have also seen children who bring objects into a classroom to share, like the little girl in Lashaunda's class who brought in a plastic box that she used as a percussion instrument. They were creating their culminating year-end performance, and this little girl loved this box she found at home and brought it in for all of her fellow students to play. She showed them how she played it and then passed it around the room so everyone else could try and discover for themselves how they wanted to make sound with it. This shows both mindfulness and generosity.

11

Better Lessons with Sound-Making

I cannot tell you how many teachers have told me after coaching sessions, workshops, or presentations at the National Association for the Education of Young Children or National Head Start Conferences that their heads are exploding with new ideas—that they can't wait to get back to school to put sound to work with transition times. All of a sudden, everything shifts, and transition times are something teachers are actually looking forward to doing with their students!

Working with sound invigorates teachers and provides opportunities for them to stretch their creativity and imagination and figure out their own wonderful ways to incorporate sound into their everyday instruction. Take, for example, the choo choo train Sound Sculpture that my friend Rachel came up with. She was working with some pre-K teachers who needed to walk their students from the classroom to the cafeteria, at least a five-minute or more transition. Her idea was a simple approach to having the students make the sound of what a choo choo train sound likes while they make the journey to the cafeteria and back. As you can imagine, everyone was engaged and focused on making the sounds quietly; no one was running away, and everyone stayed in line (see the choo choo train Sound Sculpture in the Quick Start Guide).

I also remember going into Kathy's class many years ago. Kathy was an excellent veteran pre-K teacher who suffered no fools. She didn't know anything about me other then I was in Detroit as part of the PNC Grow Up Great Initiative, and here comes this guy from New York City to help pre-K teachers teach. Anyway, I can still hear were words to me as she introduced me to her students and then turned to me and said, "Go ahead, teach me something, show me what you got." Well, the reason she's the kind of teacher I love and have the greatest respect for regardless that her attitude toward me was negative or personal; it was because as soon as she saw I had her students in the palm of my hand within 15 seconds, engaged, focused, making all kinds of great sounds and silences, laughing, and learning most of all, all she wanted to do was to learn how to do that for herself.

Pre-K teachers teach because they have a calling to do so, and with that same spirit, I have been driven to transform this information into a system and method that every teacher, parent, and caregiver can easily embrace and use with their children. The only limitations of engaging with sounds and silences are the ones we impose upon ourselves. Every lesson, curriculum, or subject matter that you use and want to teach your students can be enhanced and transformed into fun, play-based learning through sound. All it takes is your own creativity, inspiration, ingenuity, openness, and drive to be the best teacher you can be for yourself and your students.

Part B

Implementing Creative Sound Play

12

Developing Executive Functions Using the Five Primary Elements of Sound

Engaging intentional sound-making by using any of the five Primary Elements of Sound builds, develops, and enhances EF skills–inhibitory control and self-regulation, working memory, creativity, and cognitive flexibility.

A simple example of this is counting aloud from one to ten using the five Primary Elements of Sound:

- ♦ Pitch
- ♦ Volume
- ♦ Duration (length)
- ♦ Texture
- ♦ Recognizable tempo, rhythmic beat, or freely sounded out like a leaf blowing in the wind

Whether the sound is performed freely or within a recognizable rhythmic beat, pattern, or tempo, each one of the following examples and variations can be used as a transition activity in itself.

For focusing on pitch, let's count from one to ten and alternate between a high pitch sound and low pitch sound. The number 1 is high in pitch; the number 2 is low in pitch; the number 3 is high in pitch; the number 4 is low in pitch, and so on.

Now, simply count again but reverse the pitches going from low to high. One is low in pitch; two is high in pitch; three is low, and so on.

Now, let's only focus on volume and gain control and mastery from sounding out quiet to medium to loud:

Counting from one to ten, start very quietly in a whisper and gradually get louder and louder until the class is at its loudest point when sounding the number 10. Be sure to keep a steady pace or tempo and not speed up.

It is important that the number 1 should be extremely quiet, the number 5 at a medium volume, and the number 10 at the loudest volume. Also, the beauty of this example is that as the sound gets louder, the texture of the voice will change from a whisper to a medium-sounding voice to a loud, yelling, aggressive voice.

This is similar to how we might experience a train, bus, or car coming toward us from a distance where it is very quiet at first, and then, as it gets closer and closer, it gets louder and louder until it's at its loudest point as it passes right in front of us.

Also, you may notice that as your students get louder and then quieter, the pitch of the counting will rise and fall too. Being able to sound a steady, consistent pitch while counting and getting louder and then quieter is very difficult to do, counterintuitive, and makes for an excellent challenge of its own.

Now, let's focus on duration (length) and count from one to ten and make sure to sound out all of the numbers short in duration and that there is silence or space in between each number. It is important to maintain the count as you originally did: slowly, with a consistent, steady recognizable pulse and tempo.

The second time counting from one to ten, sound out all the numbers but now long in duration and fill up the silence and space with the sound of the number. Again, it is important to maintain the count as you originally did: slowly, with a consistent, steady recognizable pulse.

For the next level use the same consistent, steady recognizable pulse, and sound out the first five numbers, one to five, as short as possible; there should be silence and space in between each number. The next five numbers, six to ten, are long in duration with no silence or space in between. They should sound connected and flow into one another. What matters most is that the pulse, tempo, time and space in between counting each number be the same regardless of whether the number is sounded out short with silence in between or long and connected. And just so you know, most people speed up when making shorter sounds because they forget to include the space of silence in between each number, but do your best not to.

After all of your students can execute counting from one to ten while sounding out the numbers as short and long sounds, add what we did with volume into the mix and go from quiet to medium to loud while sounding out one to five as short and six to ten as long.

And finally, to complete this entire exercise, do all of the variations as we did but in reverse by counting down from ten to one, and then put it together by counting forward and backward. And don't be overwhelmed, part of the magic is that each one of these ways of counting is a transition activity unto itself that you and your students can use, practice and repeat many, many, many times.

There are tons of standard academic exercises that you do with your students on a daily basis that you can now begin to integrate the five Primary Elements of Sound—high or low pitch, how loud or quiet, how long or short, type of texture, and if performed freely or with a pattern, pulse, or beat of some kind. Use your imagination and have fun integrating them. Some standard academic exercises may work better with some Sound Activities than others. Always be deliberate and introduce them slowly. Sound out a sentence of words. Do it quietly, then at a medium volume, and then loudly. Do it slowly, then get faster and faster, and then gradually get slower and slower. Sound all the words long and then short. Use accents on certain syllables and make others quiet.

As you begin to work with sound and all of its aspects, it will become much easier for you and your students. Start simply and slowly, and as mastery is attained, add variations and layers of complexity. Use these layers of complexity as reinforcing exercises and repeat them as warm-ups, cooldowns, and transition games and tools. Be creative and thoughtful, and if you can manage it, keep a log of which Sound Activities and exercises resonate and work best for you. You can come back to them over and over again.

Never forget that children love to actively make sound and silence and that making sound requires no skill, additional knowledge, or language skills, just the sheer joy of making sound.

Most importantly, the more you work with sound with your students, the more aware of sound they will become. The more aware of sound, the greater the ability they will achieve to master working with sound. The more they master, the more engaged they will become. The more engaged and confident they become as ensemble players, the greater their desire will be to take agency, gain independence, and direct the ensemble. All of these skills are directly related to enhancing the three core attributes of EF skills–inhibitory control, cognitive flexibility, and working memory, as well as increasing their ability to interact socially, improve their mindfulness and hand-eye coordination, boost their emotional wellness, and raise their self-esteem.

13

Using Variation and Added Complexity

Variation is the process of exploring a specific task in ways that lead to greater ability and understanding. It allows for an exercise to be mastered and then rearranged into more complicated variations, thus developing one's ability to gain greater technical prowess. Variations are created once a simple idea or activity can be performed effortlessly. It is at this point that it is reworked and is to be performed either backward, slowly, quickly, loudly, quietly, staccato (short sounds), legato (long sounds), in ascending or descending order, or in any other combination. Variations are often more interesting and vibrant than the original idea itself.

Keep in mind that throughout each day, there are many transition times that you have to navigate and guide your students to go through from one activity to another. The beauty of variations is that each individual variation for any of the five Primary Elements of Sound or the 12 Sound Activities can serve as wonderful transition activities that you can repeat many, many times and rely on to focus and engage your students. Counting students. Moving your students from the carpet to the tables and back again. Lining students up to go outside or to the gym. Getting their attention to begin to clean up. Keeping them in line, engaged, and focused while walking them down the hall to the cafeteria. A wonderful, stress free world of infinite possibilities to easily draw from all year long.

Examples of Variation:
   Primary Activity: Counting and Clapping
      Everyone counts aloud in a steady, slow tempo: 1, 2, 3, 4, 1, 2, 3, 4…etc., and keep repeating.
      Count out loud <u>1</u>, 2, 3, 4, <u>1</u>, 2, 3, 4, <u>1</u>, 2, 3, 4, <u>1</u>, 2, 3, 4.
      Clap only when saying the number <u>1</u>.
   Variation I:
      Count out loud 1, <u>2</u>, 3, 4, 1, <u>2</u>, 3, 4, 1, <u>2</u>, 3, 4, 1, <u>2</u>, 3, 4.
      Clap only when saying the number <u>2</u>.
   Variation II:
      Count out loud 1, 2, <u>3</u>, 4, 1, 2, <u>3</u>, 4, 1, 2, <u>3</u>, 4, 1, 2, <u>3</u>, 4.
      Clap only when saying the number <u>3</u>.
   Variation III:
      Count out loud 1, 2, 3, <u>4</u>, 1, 2, 3, <u>4</u>, 1, 2, 3, <u>4</u>, 1, 2, 3, <u>4</u>.
      Clap only when saying the number <u>4</u>.
   Variation IV:
      Count backward out loud <u>4</u>, 3, 2, 1, <u>4</u>, 3, 2, 1, <u>4</u>, 3, 2, 1.
      Clap only when saying the number 4, and so on. Clap only when saying the number 3, and so on. Clap only when saying the number 2, and so on. Clap only when saying the number 1, and so on.

Creating a Variation of a Primary Activity

But we are not limited to just counting and clapping. What about counting and stomping feet? Let's make a variation of the initial Sound Activity counting and clapping and vary it so it becomes counting and stomping.

   Counting and Stomping:
      Count out loud <u>1</u>, 2, 3, 4, <u>1</u>, 2, 3, 4, <u>1</u>, 2, 3, 4, <u>1</u>, 2, 3, 4.
      Stomp right foot only when saying the number <u>1</u>.
   Variation I:
      Count out loud <u>1</u>, 2, 3, 4, <u>1</u>, 2, 3, 4, <u>1</u>, 2, 3, 4, <u>1</u>, 2, 3, 4
      Stomp left foot only when saying the number <u>1</u>.
   Variation II:
      Count out loud 1, <u>2</u>, 3, 4, 1, <u>2</u>, 3, 4, 1, <u>2</u>, 3, 4, 1, <u>2</u>, 3, 4.
      Stomp right foot only when saying the number <u>2</u>.

Variation III:
> Stomp left foot only when saying the number 2.
> Adding Complexity to a Variation:

Integrating Counting, Clapping, and Stomping:
> Count out loud 1, 2, 3, 4, 1, 2, 3, 4, 1, 2, 3, 4, 1, 2, 3, 4.
> Clap only when saying the number 1.
> Stomp right foot only when saying the number 3.

Variation I:
> Clap only when saying the number 2.
> Stomp right foot only when saying the number 4.

Variation II:
> Clap only when saying the number 2.
> Stomp right foot only when saying the number 3.

Variation III:
> Stomp right foot only when saying the number 1.
> Clap only when saying the number 4, and so on.
> Adding Additional Complexity to a Variation Clapping, Stomping, and Vocal Accent:
> Count out loud 1, 2, 3, 4, 1, 2, 3, 4, 1, 2, 3, 4, 1, 2, 3, 4.
> Clap on 1, say 2 in a high-pitched voice, and stomp on 4.

Variation I:
> Count out loud 1, 2, 3, 4, 1, 2, 3, 4, 1, 2, 3, 4, 1, 2, 3, 4.
> Whisper on 1, clap loudly on 3, stomp softly on 4.

Variation II:
> Count out loud 1, 2, 3, 4, 1, 2, 3, 4, 1, 2, 3, 4, 1, 2, 3, 4.
> Say 1 in a low voice, rub hands on 2, and stomp both feet on 4.

Adding More Variation:
> Now, do the same exercises, but count backward.
>> Change the interval that is counted to and count to 3—1, 2, 3, 1, 2, 3, 1, 2, 3—and begin simply with clapping only on 1. Then clap on 2, then on 3, and so forth.
>> Change the type of sound and add different types of clapping (see the technique and texture Sound Activity): flat clap, monster clap, applause clap, pat clap.
>> Change the interval and count to 5—1, 2, 3, 4, 5, 1, 2, 3, 4, 5—and begin again by placing one clap on one number. Change that up and add a stomp, etc.

And finally, of course, if you want to include making all kinds of crazy funny vocal sounds, you can do that too. Why not add animal sounds, a dog's bark, a cow's moo, a cat's meow, an owl's hoot, a wolf's howl, a pig's oink, a horse's neigh, and a lion's roar. Most importantly, have fun because the possibilities are truly endless for creating playful, engaging variations with and for your students, who will absolutely love and adore all of this!

14

The 12 Sound Activities

1. Counting, Clapping, and Stomping

Gain the ability to count and perform a deliberately controlled clap, stomp, or both on a given number(s), beat, or pattern.

2. Technique and Texture

Develop the controlled ability to deliberately create sounds that produce different types of textures. For now, we will only use our hands to generate sound.

Clapping:
There are four basic ways to clap hands, each making a different kind of clap sound and texture, and two basic ways to rub hands:
Flat Clap – this is when both hands are flat, much like hands in prayer. This type of clap produces a relatively crisp sound without much resonance.
Monster Clap – this is when both hands are at right angles to each other (or cross), cupped, and create an air pocket that when clapped creates a more hollow, resonant, deep sound.
Applause Clap – this is similar to the monster clap, where both hands are at right angles to each other, but here, the fingers are closed and strike the palm of the other hand.

This type of clap allows for the greatest range of volume—from quiet to loud while still maintaining a rich, resonant sound.

Pat Clap – this is when one hand gently pats the other hand and tends to make the lightest, quietest sound of all four types of claps.

Rubbing:

Back and Forth Rub – this produces a two-stroke sound. One can do this with just the hands or use hands to rub arms, legs, etc.

Round Rub – this creates a circular sound that seems to go on forever. One can do this with just hands or hands that rub arms, tummies, legs, etc.

3. Dynamic Control

The ability to create controlled sound at variable levels of volume—quiet, medium, and loud.

4. Emphasis, Duration, and Pitch

The ability to deliberately control how a sound will sound. It is exactly like how we speak and choose to accentuate and emphasize or not emphasize words or parts of words and syllables in a sentence to convey the meaning, and emotional sentiment of what we are expressing. Duration is the length of sound, whether short, medium, or long, and pitch means high, low, and everything in between.

5. Time and Tempo

This means simply gaining the ability to control tempo, whether by keeping a steady tempo or by purposely speeding it up or purposely slowing it down. This is a matter of simply understanding how sounds and silences interact in time. For all of you who feel you have no rhythm, that is false. We all have hearts; they beat in "rhythm" or time, and the heart is the first drum.

So for keeping a steady tempo, can you count for the duration of one second? Of course, you can: say out loud 1 potato. That is about the same length as one second of sound. Now say 1 potato, 2 potato, and you have now just counted the equivalent of how long two seconds last.

Now, simply count 1 potato, 2 potato, 3 potato, 4 potato, and clap your hands every time you say the number. This is a steady tempo and is roughly one beat per second. Repeat this slowly a few times and get comfortable. There is no rush nor any judgment. Everyone is completely capable of this, and the more you practice this with your students, the easier it will become. And don't forget, your students will love it. Just think of all the complex words that have several syllables you can use to practice with: 1 banana, 2 banana, 3 banana, 4 banana…1 papaya, 2 papaya, 3 papaya, 4 papaya. And to make the tempo even a little slower, add more syllables: 1 pepperoni pizza, 2 pepperoni pizza, 3 pepperoni pizza, and so on.

And for faster tempos that you want to keep constant, just count fewer syllables. For example, repeat what we just did earlier and count at the same speed, clapping only when you say the number: 1 potato, 2 potato, 3 potato, 4 potato. Now keep counting at the same speed, but just count 1 po, 2 po, 3 po, 4 po, and clap on every number. Presto, you have a constant tempo that is just about twice as fast as the one when counting 1 potato, 2 potato, 3 potato, 4 potato. It's all about the amount of syllables you count.

So now let's have a blast going between the potato and po clapping only on the numbers: 1 potato, 2 potato, 1 po, 2 po, 3 po, 4 po, 1 potato, 2 potato, 1 po, 2 po, 3 po, 4 po.

And finally, once you have mastered counting the numbers and syllables out loud at a slow tempo while you clap on a given number or syllable, switch it up and count the numbers and syllables but now only in your head. You can continue to move your lips, bob your head, and even tap your foot lightly as you count only in your head, just don't make any sound. Then clap your hands on a given number or syllable and hear how steady your clapping sound is. Who says you don't have rhythm?

6. Passing a Clap One-to-One

This is the ability to move a sound from one person to another, one at a time. It is much like the game "telephone" that we played as kids, but here only with sound.

The other aspect to listen for is trying to make the amount of silence on either side of a clap even. Allow yourself to experiment with this without judgment. This is probably the most zen aspect of sound because it's all about trusting the silence. From my experience, most people clap and then shortchange the silence and rush to make the next clap. Try not to shortchange the silence, which is just as important if not more important than the clap sound. Silence allows for a pause and a breadth and defines the space around the sound. Trust that you will hear it.

7. Dividing the Class into Groups

This is about dividing the ensemble—or class—into smaller parts to create more deliberately organized types of sounds that can be played at any time. This immediately lends itself to more complexity when creating sound: adding counterpoint, different types of textures, etc. Divide the class into two, three, four, or more groups to create Team A, Team B, Team C, Team D, etc.

How to learn the different parts:

> It is always best to have the class as a whole play, learn, and practice all of the individual parts prior to dividing the class into teams. Once everyone can perform the individual parts easily, it is time to divide the class into the number of teams or parts that are to be played. Before having the whole class play together, it is very important that each team be able to practice and play their parts alone while the other team waits quietly and listens. Once everyone is comfortable with their separate parts, it is time to put them together as a full ensemble. The last element of this Sound Activity is that all of the teams should have the opportunity to play all of the different individual parts separately and together.

8. Improvising and Creating Dialogue

This is creating a conversation with abstract sound that two or more people actively participate in. Much like a conversation with words but now only with sounds.

9. Rhythmic Literacy

This is applying two basic traditional music notation symbols to actively make sound and silence. The first is a quarter note, which is the equivalent of one beat of sound and looks like this with either its stem going up.

Stem going up

Or

Stem going down

Depending on the direction of the stem going up or down, it makes it possible to assign a quarter note symbol to represent two different types of sounds. The stem going up is a clap, and the stem going down a stomp. The stem going up is a dog's bark, and the stem going down a duck's quack. Whatever you and your students want it to be.

The second traditional music notation symbol is a quarter note rest, which is the equivalent of one beat of rest or silence and looks like this.

A quarter note rest

It is imperative to understand that playing silence is as important, if not more important, than playing sound. Remember, silence is an active task and in actuality is what gives shape and importance to all sound. Therefore, silence is a deliberate action and intention that we create, And finally, Cecilia, a wonderful teacher at the Lenox Hill Neighborhood House Early Childhood Center, inspired her 3-year-olds to apply color to the quarter note symbols, making them even more dynamic. Her students together decided that because red, yellow, and orange are hot colors, quarter notes in those colors should be played as loud sounds, while quarter notes in blue, purple, and green—the cool colors—should be played as quiet sounds.

Not only did Cecilia's students, over two or three weeks of practice, master sight-reading sound phrases that included quarter notes (a beat of sound) and quarter note rests (a beat of silence), but they interpreted two different levels of volume depending on the color of the quarter note, and two different types of sound depending on the direction of the quarter note stems—up or down. They first sounded it all out by clapping and stomping and then transferred and performed the same notated sound phrases using two handheld percussion instruments in a performance.

See Chapter 21, Week 9, for more examples.

10. Art Sounds

Art Sounds is simply using your students' artwork—drawings, paintings, collages, papier-mâché, constructions, assemblages, or sculptures—as a prompt to organize, interpret, compose, and perform sound. I have tried this many times and believe me, it is one of the most fun and free Creative Sound Play exercises. For the most part, it should be left up to the children to decide how the artwork will sound, but as always it is helpful to offer some guidelines. One teacher suggested that the number of colors used should determine the volume of the sounds performed. One color equaled a quiet (soft or hushed) sound, two colors were to be played at a medium or ordinary volume, and three colors or more produced loud, exuberant sounds (Figure 14.1). In addition to teaching students how to modulate their sound and expression, this encouraged counting and visual discrimination, leading students to look at their art in a whole new way and how they may want to tell a story.

By pointing at or holding up a painting for 10 or so seconds, in any order, a child can have their paintings performed by the ensemble (class).

But why stop at color as a prompt when there is so much more in art that can inspire thoughtful, meaningful sound? What if anything is being depicted? What are the different colors? How was the paint applied? Are the marks round or straight, short or long? These are all elements that can be used as prompts to help students create a host of fun, deliberate, and intentional sounds. Let's examine these three finger paintings to see what I mean.

Quiet (soft)　　　　**Medium**　　　　**Loud**

FIGURE 14.1 Art Sounds

First, take the blue painting, which was sounded as "Quiet" because it had only one color. But what about paint application? Don't those round swirls suggest the quiet sound that comes from rubbing hands together in a circular motion, as we learned earlier in the Technique and Texture Sound Activity? This painting could also inspire quiet, repeated vocal sounds, for example running words together to create a "spinning" sound: Wish-You, Wish-You, Wish-You etc. This can be a lot of fun, especially when you start playing around with the speed or tempo by slowing down or speeding up the Wish-You, Wish-You, Wish-You, or You-Wish, You-Wish, You-Wish. Once the students are making theses sounds, try having them close their eyes to let go of the visual prompt and experience just hearing the sound itself as a texture filling the room.

The middle painting was sounded at "Medium" volume because it used two colors, blue and magenta. Another way to approach such a painting would be to divide your class in two (or let them choose) and have each half sound one of the colors. Then have the two groups take turns, passing their sounds back and forth, at first simply and then with overlaps – the sound for blue begins, then lingers and slowly diminishes as the magenta sound enters and takes center stage, lingers, and then fades away in turn as the sound for blue begins a new cycle. Plus, since the finger marks in both the blue and magenta colors resemble a variety of different lengths of strokes, so should the durations of the all the sounds. This will also call everyone's attention to what happens at the important part of the painting where the two colors meet. And needless to say, this exercise would provide a wonderful opportunity for students to conduct the class.

Finally, the painting on the right was sounded as "Loud" because it had three or more colors. But look: it also consists of oval type, multi-colored dots with space or "Silence" between them. This punctuated structure makes it perfect for the four types of claps we've already learned: flat, monster, applause, and pat claps. After going over the four types, have each student clap once and then stop, wait, and create space by playing silence before they clap again. The element of chance in this group activity will be lots of fun as the claps bump into each other or try to stay out of each other's way. Then, to add complexity to the sound palette, offer your students stomps and short vocal sounds as well.

In addition to these whole-class activities, try dividing your class into groups and assign each group a different painting to sound out. Let the groups know that after discussing and coming up with their own approach, they will be able to share it with the class and get feedback. And for variety or to extend the activity, switch up the groups and paintings.

Of course, there are many other factors that can be brought into consideration: shapes and directions of lines, their thicknesses, the density of images, the areas of the artwork left untouched or blank, and the kinds of materials used, such as colored paper, tissue paper, crayons, paint, pencils, tape, string, buttons, cork, bottle caps, sparkles, etc. All of these can and do suggest sound. You can use artworks that have already been made or ask your students to make art knowing that it will become part of a sound piece. And don't forget, just as a piece of music can have different sections or movements, a sound piece can be triggered by one artwork or several, it's all up to the child.

11. Conducting through Patterns

This is using one's fingers, hands, and/or arms to physically outline a specific pattern or shape through the air that shows the tempo and number of counts for the ensemble or class to follow. See Chapter 21, Week 11 (see p. 142), "Conducting through Patterns" for diagrams.

12. Conducting through Gesture

This is freely using any kind of physical gesture to indicate where sound begins and ends, it's volume(s), how dense, who plays sound at any given time, etc.

15

Transferring the 12 Sound Activities to Hand Percussion Instruments

The next level of working with Creative Sound Play is transferring all of the 12 Sound Activities previously learned with body parts and voices to a variety of handheld percussion instruments—drums, hand drums, shakers, cymbals, finger cymbals, triangles, tambourines, wood blocks, guiros, bells, hand bells, cowbells, claves, and maracas. This assortment of hand percussion instruments represents a wonderful variety of sounds and textures to work with, much like a small orchestra.

Most importantly now, do not get overwhelmed. These hand percussion instruments are nothing more than sound makers and should only be considered as such. As you approach them, remember the five Primary Elements of Sound—pitch, volume, duration, texture, and either playing freely or with a recognizable pattern, beat or tempo.

Regarding texture, like our hands with clapping and rubbing, there are different ways to approach playing each hand percussion instrument. Each approach will produce a different type of sound. Do not restrict yourself as to how you think they are only to be played correctly. Pretend you are one of your students or that you are from another planet where none of these instruments (sound makers) exist and that you are seeing them all for the first time. Take some time with each one and experiment with them. Hit, strike, rub, pat, shake, and tap them all in different ways. Hold them in different ways. Muffle the instruments and hear and listen to how the sound changes. See which instruments make short sounds and which make longer ones that take time to ring off. For instruments with skins, experiment with pressing down on their skins or "heads" with your thumbs while hitting, striking, or patting them and hear how the sound changes depending on the amount of pressure you have pressing against the skin. Experiment, experiment, experiment, and then experiment some more! Have fun. The only wrong way to play these instruments is to abuse them, which I am sure you will never ever do.

Now, turn your kids loose with the instruments and see how inventive they are with how to play them. Let them just experiment to their hearts' delight. After a while, challenge them to make quiet sounds. Then silence, then loud sounds, then silence, then medium sounds. Divide the class into two groups and have one play and then the other wait and listen, one group at a time. Have your students demonstrate different ways of playing each instrument. Have your students sit in a circle, each with one instrument, and have them play the instrument and pass the sound around the room one at a time. Listen to all the different types of sounds as they sound one after another, each with a completely different texture. Some, by the nature of their instrument, will be louder than others. And some, by their nature, will make longer sounds than others. Make all of these instruments your friends and develop the ability and control to be able to play each one in a variety of ways by hitting, tapping, rubbing, shaking, scraping, turning them upside down, using different parts of your hands and fingers—anything you can think of that may produce different kinds of textures of sounds. Have your students do the same and explain how the different ways of playing them creates a different kind of sound and texture.

As you all gain more familiarity with these hand percussion instruments, play, and perform all of the 12 Sound Activities slowly and thoroughly, always paying great attention to performing with focus, control, and intention. It is also very important to make sure that everyone has the opportunity to play all of the various types of instruments.

As well, now that all of your students are well versed with the 12 Sound Activities, it is time for them to take control to lead and decide which sound activities to work on at any given point. Also, see how they may want to challenge themselves by adding greater complexity to the activity.

Because logistically, it requires more time to work with the handheld percussion instruments, it is understood that you may not be able to do so on a daily basis. The next best level would be working with them three or four times a week. If that is too much, then twice a week will suffice. What is most important is that you continue the daily practice of using all five Primary Elements of Sound—pitch, volume, duration, texture—and whether the sound is performed freely or within a recognizable rhythmic beat, pattern, or tempo, and the 12 Sound Activities as short, fun, transition learning bursts.

16

Creating Sound Sculptures for Public Performance

I'm sure by now you and your students are having a blast with creating sound and silence, and in many ways, here is where the magic of Creative Sound Play really comes alive. Because now we're going to bring everything we've been working on together to create Sound Sculptures!

Sound Sculptures are sound compositions that give sound and silence a shape or contour that evolves and unfolds over time. They have a recognizable beginning, middle, and end, and can typically last from 1 to 5 minutes or even more depending on their shape and complexity. They can be one Sound Activity or a sequence of connected Sound Activities that are either pre-determined or improvised in real time.

Sound Sculptures draw from all of the ways you and your students have been engaging with sound by varying pitch, volume, duration, texture, and tempo or no tempo. Or using all or any of the 12 Sound Activities, the Quick Start Guide, narrative ideas, or your standard curricula and favorite subject matter.

Sounds can be generated by using body parts, percussion instruments, and voices, which can include words, numbers, letters, syllables, animal sounds, etc. You can include interpretive movement and narration. You can divide the class into groups or have the whole class play together. You can have soloists.

Anything and any way you and your class want to create deliberate sound in intentional ways!

All of this is a group effort, so make sure to solicit input from your entire class during the creative process. It is also a fantastic opportunity for you to encourage your students to lead the proceedings, whether it's an entire sound sculpture or just one section.

It may seem like a lot at first, but if you just stop to think for a moment, by now, you and your students are so familiar with making sounds and silences that creating Sculptures will be a snap. And as always, most importantly, have fun and take your time. Once Sculptures are created, you can rehearse them with your students and perform them for an audience of their peers, family, and friends.

One last, incredibly important note: if you're preparing for a public performance, it's easy for everyone, kids and teachers alike, to forget one of Creative Sound Play's most important tenets: This is all about play and having fun, and it's totally okay to mess up. The only thing that matters is that everyone is trying their best!

Four Examples of Sound Sculptures

- The Choo-Choo Train Sound Sculpture. See the Quick Start Guide
- A Sound Sculpture in Three Sections
- Passing a Sound One-to-One with Volume
- Art Sounds

EXAMPLE 2   A Sound Sculpture in Three Sections

Total length 2½ to 3 minutes
Form = Three sections: A, B, and C

- Section A = 1 minute in duration
    - Conducted by Gesture.
    - Starts out very quietly.
    - The conductor points to instruments to stagger entrances one at a time, (in 2 second intervals) until everyone is playing. Then they are conducted by

gesture into a loud, frenzied texture that lasts for ten seconds to a very sharp cut-off as the conductor signals to stop making sound. Suddenly, there is a loud, abrupt silence.
- Five seconds of this silence flows seamlessly into Section B.
- Section B = 30 seconds in duration: counting pattern one to four
    - Divide class into four groups: drums, shakers, vocalists, triangles.
    - The conductor slowly counts aloud and physically makes the pattern for counting: 1, 2, 3, 4, 1, 2, 3, 4, 1, etc. Repeats and sets the tempo for the ensemble to follow.
    - Everyone begins counting along in their heads, not out loud, following the conductor: 1, 2, 3, 4, 1, 2, 3, 4, 1, etc.
    - Drums make one sound altogether when they count the number 1 in their head on beat 1 at a medium volume and rest for beats 2, 3, and 4.
    - Shakers only shake on beat 2 as loud as possible.
    - Vocalists sound the word "yes" for the full duration of beat 3, start quietly and very quickly get loud.
    - Triangles sound only on beat 4
    - Conductor continues to count 1, 2, 3, 4, 1, 2, 3, 4, 1, etc., until they are done and want to stop and move on to Section C of the Sound sculpture.
- Section C = 1 minute in duration
    - Play Section A backward—retrograde.
    - The conductor indicates everyone to start playing loudly, and then the ensemble begins to gradually get quieter; the conductor slowly indicates (in 10-second intervals) which specific instruments should stop playing until no one is playing and making any sound any longer and all are creating silence.

EXAMPLE 3   Passing a Sound One-to-One with Volume

Total length 2 to 3 minutes
Form = One section

- Set the class in a circle, each student with a different hand percussion instrument, and pass a sound around the circle. Only one instrument can sound at a time. There should be no instruments of the same kind lined up next to each other.
- Keep a steady, slow tempo, passing a sound around the circle for 15 seconds at a quiet volume. Then, keeping the same slow tempo, take 30 to 45 seconds to gradually go from everyone playing very quietly to loud, and then take 30 to 45 seconds for everyone to gradually go from playing loud to quiet.
- Speed up and slow down too. Do this for 2 minutes and then end.

EXAMPLE 4   Art Sounds

Total length 3 to 5 minutes
    Based on images Quiet, Medium, and Loud (see figure 14.1 p. 67)
    Form = Images are conducted in any order, all must be played, and each is to last for 30 to 60 seconds in duration. The very last image to end must be Quiet
    Types of sounds and textures to accompany paintings:

- Quiet = Hands rubbing in circles or running words together to create a "spinning" sound: Wish-You, Wish-You, Wish-You, and You-Wish, You-Wish, You-Wish
- Medium = Two types of textures of sounds, one for blue which will be metallic sounds—triangles, bells and finger cymbals, and the other for magenta which will be

shakers—egg shakers, maracas, and beans in plastic bottles. Divide your class in two groups and have each sound one of the colors. Then have the two groups take turns, passing their sounds back and forth, at first simply and then with overlaps—the sound for blue begins, then lingers and slowly diminishes as the magenta sound enters and takes center stage, lingers, and then fades away in turn as the sound for blue begins a new cycle. Because the finger marks in both the blue and magenta colors resemble a variety of different lengths of strokes, so should the durations of the all the sounds.

- Loud = Short Sounds ONLY—Hand drums, crash cymbals, cow bells, tambourines, wood blocks, four types of clapping hands (monster, flat, applause and pat), feet stomping and short vocal sounds. THE RULE for Loud ONLY—Play one loud sound and then stop, pause, and create space by playing a BIG silence before playing another loud sound. All sounds and silences are to be determined freely by the child.

Part C

Creative Sound Play and Special Needs

17

The History of Creative Sound Play through Special Needs

Because all children love and adore making sound, silence, and listening, it makes no difference if a child has special needs or not. Sound simply does what it does and transforms into a profound educational tool that develops EFs, SEL, active listening skills, mindfulness, reflection, agency, independence, and raises self-esteem. It's not what a child can't do that makes the difference; it's what a child can do, and making an intentional sound in a deliberate way is always play-based and inspires, focuses, and engages them. Sound-making is just a part of our DNA, our shared human experience, and provides ALL children with the opportunity to take agency, control their environment, and internalize that how and what they do matters.

If you are a special needs teacher, parent, or caregiver, everything in this method book about Creative Sound Play can apply to you, too, and help you teach and work with your children and students. After all, it was in my work with special needs children pre-K through high school that I first came to see and internalize how profound integrating sound-making, silence, and listening can be used as a robust, comprehensive educational method for all. To that end, this is the only chapter that differentiates between general ed and special needs children and that is only to clarify the fact that children are children, and all children love and adore Creative Sound Play.

The sole reason why I became a musician is because I love making and listening to sound. I remember when I first got my hands on a saxophone. All I would do is blow the horn in this big stairwell that had great reverberation. I would blow for hours just listening to and being totally enthralled with the sound—not the notes or lines per se, but just the sound. Ah, how my poor neighbors must have suffered!

Fast forward a few decades (who's counting?), and I'm still in love with sound. The simple act of creating and organizing sound has given my life focus, purpose, and meaning. Over the years, I have worked with special needs children of all ages who have all kinds of challenges—autism, attention-deficit/hyperactivity, intellectual disabilities, learning disabilities, sensory processing disorder, physical disabilities, emotional and behavioral problems, speech, language, and developmental delays, and Down Syndrome.

It was working with high-functioning special needs high school students that enabled me the insight to see the profound educational impact making and listening to sound and silence can have on teaching all children, period!

In 2005, Lori, an amazing special needs education teacher at a public special needs high school in Queens, New York, asked me to present a music workshop for her students. After some discussion, we decided that a "Sound and Silence" intensive residency—working every day for ten days with her students—was the way to go. Our goal was to have all of her students experience what it is to make sound and be a part of an instrumental ensemble that communicates with each other by making abstract sounds.

Throughout the residency, everyone focused and engaged in actively making sounds using flute-o-phones in deliberate ways. Flute-o-phones are recorder-like instruments that are not as loud or shrill sounding as traditional recorders, so for autistic kids, it's much easier on their ears. More importantly, everyone intently listened to each other's sounds and silences, making it possible to really create a fulfilling sound experience. It was quite beautiful and meaningful for all of us, so much so that all of Lori's students became self-motivated and continued making sound together even after my participation had ended.

Here is an email I received from Lori the week after my ten-day workshop ended:

> The QOTC is experiencing Hayes withdrawal...the kids came in today and made a beeline for their flutophones even before hanging up their coats. I was on the telephone with a parent and they just got started—Keith and Brandon were having a musical conversation and Ella started helping Jasmine move her fingers to make different sounds. Lewis dragged the snare drum and a set of bongos over to the tables and got DaShaun to play. It was wild, they started jamming-reminding each other to listen and to play the silence! I sat back a watched them take ownership-admittedly got teary eyed at how they have embraced the experience and want more. Hayes, it is so rare that these kids take initiative, show energy to express themselves or explore things creatively on their own without step-by-step adult directives. You've brought something magic to their lives. Best of all, Francesca commented, "I liked him. He was a good reason to stay awake."

So there you have it, the ultimate compliment via Francesca.

From this experience, I realized the importance of sound and the amazing possibilities that it offers. This was the formal beginning of what would evolve into Creative Sound Play.

Over the next few years, among the countless special needs students that I've loved working with, three stand out that exemplify and illustrate the sheer power of creating deliberate and intentional sound and silence. Each student taught me profound lessons about listening to listening, and by that I mean, how much do we really hear what we hear?

Here is a chronological narrative of my experiences with Antoine, Marcos, and Benjamin.

Antoine:

In 2005, on my first day of working with Antoine and his class of wonderful 15- or 16-year-old special needs students, I had all of the kids playing flute-o-phones.

I drew a picture on the board and asked everyone to interpret it by making sound by blowing however they wanted to into their flute-o-phones. I made a few suggestions as to how I might interpret the drawing to break the ice and then asked the class to go ahead and make the sounds and silences that they felt the picture sounded like. We all had a lot of fun.

Five or ten minutes later, I erased the drawing I had made and asked Antoine to come up and draw a picture of his own that we could all interpret with our flute-o-phones. One of the adult teaching assistants in the class said, "Oh, he's a mimic," and then, somewhat disparagingly, "He can't think for himself and is just going to redraw everything that was there." Needless to say, I did not appreciate her attitude.

Well, sure enough, Antoine did exactly that, and quite meticulously, I might add. It must have taken him 5 minutes to copy my drawing and with such beautiful care. That's what touched me the most: the care in which he painstakingly redrew everything. So when he finished, I asked him how he wanted us to play it. He suggested we play it how I had originally mentioned to the class, and we did.

Now, about four or five days into the residency, the kids are all feeling comfortable with me, and that day's activities involved playing a series of call and response in pairs, two kids each with their flute-o-phones. One kid plays a short sound or a series of sounds, and their partner plays the same sound back.

I was working with Antoine. We were sitting across from each other on stools, and Antoine had no problem giving back to me what I had given him. After all, he's a "mimic." At least everyone said so, and that's what he had been told his entire life. I said to him, "Okay, Antoine, it's your turn to lead." At that point, he looked at me and said, "Oh no, I can't do that." To this I replied, "Of course you can, just give me one boop." Again, he said, "No, I can't do that." This went on several more times. Finally, I could see that I was beginning to wear him down, and so I said, "Come on, Antoine, just give me one boop. TRY IT!" Finally, he slowly began to pick up his flute-o-phone and put it to his lips. He made a very timid little boop, which I gave him back immediately. He stopped, cocked his head to one side and back a little bit, and looked at me quite surprised. I said, "Go on, Antoine, give me another boop; you can do it." Again, we went back and forth a few times until he took his time and slowly put the flute-o-phone up to his lips and made another boop, this time a little less timid. Again, I gave him a boop right back. Again, he cocks his head back a bit and to the side, but now he is beginning to feel a little empowered. I asked him to do it again and he stopped and thought about it, and then without much more hesitation, he gave me two boops, and I gave him his two boops back. At that moment, his eyes widened so far you could see the light go on in his head. All of a sudden, you could see that the world looked different to him. Just like that, for the first time in his life, he could think for himself; he was his own person, and he could lead. He stood up, came over to me, and gave me the biggest, warmest hug.

Who knew and who knows what happened right there in Antoine's head and what kind of impact that had on him, perhaps for the rest of his life? What I do know is that all it took was the care to listen to him and challenge him with something that he thought he was completely incapable of doing. And isn't that what we all need?

Marcos:

A year later, I was working with a group of special ed teachers, assistant teachers, and their special ed students. I was giving a hands-on workshop/demonstration so that the teachers could learn firsthand how using sound play and making intentional sound in deliberate ways could help them teach and impact their students in so many great ways. There were about 14 or 16 teachers and 24 students, and I went twice a week for three or four weeks.

So, Marcos was this skinny, nonverbal kid who was about 16 or 17 years old and was forever getting into trouble for making all kinds of noises and disrupting his classes. He had absolutely NO inhibitory control whatsoever—none! Plus, he did not speak, or, more accurately, he made all kinds of vocal sounds galore, but had such a big, warm smile and so much charisma everyone loved him and let him get away with it all. As far as anyone there knew, no one had ever heard him speak or sound out a word of English or Spanish, and he had been a student there for two or three years.

So, of course, when we were using the flute-o-phones, he was just blown away and having a ball with himself the whole time. Meanwhile, he's finally beginning to get on my nerves. As usual, I looked for the most difficult kids to work with, and Marcos was my man. At this point, I was conducting the kids by physical gestures, indicating when and when not to play, as well as how loud or softly to play. I looked at Marcos and told him that he was now going to be my soloist, which I explained was a very important position to have, and that he must wait quietly in his chair playing silence (not making a sound) until I instructed him through gesture by pointing at him to stand up and let it wail and blow to his heart's content. And then when I felt his job as soloist was over, I would gesture to him to sit back down in his chair and go back to playing silence. After all, I was now Maestro Hayes!

Well, Marcos was amazing! As hard as he struggled to hold back, he did so and with such grace. Everyone could see and feel his struggle as he squirmed around in his chair, gripping the flute-o-phone and not playing it. As hard as it was for him, I know it was harder for us looking on. And when, after about 2 minutes or so of him holding back and playing silence, I finally instructed him to play sound, and he jumped up and just let it rip. He blew the roof off with that flute-o-phone. It was thrilling. He filled the room with sheer enthusiasm and excitement. And then when I gestured for him to sit back down and play silence, he did so effortlessly.

If that wasn't profound enough to witness, what totally blew everyone's mind next that day was when, after pointing out what an excellent job Marcos had performed as a soloist to his peers and teachers and had everyone applaud, I asked the class who wanted to come up and conduct, and before anyone could respond, Marcos's hand shot up in the air first, and he yelled out without hesitation and with complete authority, "I do, I want to conduct!" I must have had two or three teachers, one of whom was crying, ask me how did I do that.

Benjamin:

Here was this kid, about 16 or 17 years old and maybe 300 pounds or so of what looked to be solid muscle. This kid looked like a football linebacker. He was wide and thick. Not tall, and not fat, just wide and thick. Not only that, but he also looked at me with anger, disdain, and meanness. Clearly, this was the last place on earth at that moment that Benjamin ever wanted to be, and he seriously scared me. He could have broken me in two with a flick of one hand.

On his first day, Benjamin came to class late with his assistant teacher. The rest of us were in a semicircle, spread out in a fairly large classroom. He grabbed a chair and placed it up against the far wall so that he was about 20 feet away from the closest student. He sat squarely in the chair with his arms folded across his chest and faced the wall, almost pressed up against it. He was angry, and there could not have been more than two inches between his nose and that wall.

At this point in the workshop, we were passing the sound of one handclap around the room, one-to-one. Since Benjamin clearly wasn't interested in participating, and he scared me a bit, I decided that he should just be left alone to his own devices. Well, I don't think that the sound went around the room more than once, if that, before Benjamin jumped up, clapped his hands once, and joined the class. From that moment on, everything changed for him. He participated, had a smile, was a pleasure to be around, took the seat next to me, and became my wingman. On one of the following days, while in class with everyone, I heard him tapping his fingers on his chair. I asked him why he was making that sound, and he said it sounded like tap dancing. I asked the class if anyone knew what tap dancing was, and none did. I asked Benjamin if he wouldn't mind demonstrating what tap dancing was for the class. He was more than happy to oblige and proceeded to happily tap dance the best he could around the room. It was beautiful to see, especially because he was so wide and thick and was wearing sneakers, so everyone, including Marcos, had to be really quiet to hear the sound of his feet tap dancing across the floor. By the end of the workshop, Benjamin was leading the class with sounds, silences, and singing.

So how much of what we hear do we really hear, and how does making and creating sounds and silence with deliberate intention provide such powerful, meaningful, and profound tools to work with?

For Antoine, the simple action of leading by deliberately blowing on a flute-o-phone and having someone else respond to him rocked his world and awakened within him a new self-image and perspective on how to live—to see and understand that he has the power and ability to think for himself, can lead and make choices, and that he makes a difference in this world.

For Marcos, instead of fighting and pleading with him to be quiet and then scolding him when he was not, simply providing a fun, joyful context in which he could deliberately create intentional silences and sounds helped him to experience what inhibitory control is, so much so that it inspired him to speak words for the first time in that setting in order to get a chance to enjoy the role of leader. Creative Sound Play is a simple tool that now, in the hands of teachers, can help children like Marcos grow and experience that how and what they do matters in the world in so many basic, beautiful, and unknown ways that can impact their EF abilities, SEL, mindfulness, active listening skills, and so much more.

As for Benjamin, just having a context in which he could express himself and be creative with just pure sound and silence and to be respected and listened to without judgment enabled him to open up, share his knowledge, socialize, and become a full-fledged active participant.

And all this just by making sound and silence.

Part D

Daily and Yearly Calendar, and Schedule for Working with Sound

18

Approaching the School Year

I am sure that over time, you have learned and honed many skills that help you teach. As with everything, time, attention, and consistent practice are the sole determinants of real success and mastery.

Understanding how the process for learning Creative Sound Play and sound and silence unfolds within the school year is very useful.

- ♦ The first third of the year is devoted solely to mastering the Quick Start Guide, which enables teachers and students to develop a strong foundation for the first three Primary Elements of Sound—pitch, volume, and duration—using only our voices and bodies as the source for making sound used for transition activities.
- ♦ The second third is trifold—continuing the sound transitions as a regular teaching routine, learning more types of Sound Activities, and then transferring that same information to now include external sound makers: a variety of handheld percussion instruments.
- ♦ The last few months of the school year are dedicated to Sound Sculpturing—creating and organizing stories and compositions with your students. Sound Sculptures utilize all of the information we have learned, and they can be rehearsed and, more importantly, publicly performed for fellow students, parents, families, and friends.

♦ Throughout the year, it is important that teachers track their students so that as soon as students take agency of a Sound Activity, they can shift from leader to facilitator and encourage all of their students to participate in deciding how Sound Activities sound as well as lead them.

In your first year of implementing Creative Sound Play, I suggest you work with only those Sound Activities that really resonate most with you. Allow yourself to investigate them in all kinds of ways. Always remember that as long as you are deliberate with your intention, there is no wrong way of making sound and silence. With regular, daily, and consistent play, you and your students will become masters of sound-making.

In truth, at first, it is not how many of the 12 Sound Activities you and your students can perform the simple basics of that count and make the difference but how thoroughly fluent and masterful you and your children become with those few Sound Activities you choose to work with consistently throughout the school year. It is only through this process of focus, consistent practice, and adding variations of complexity to those few Sound Activities that will enable you to really see, understand, and experience how sound and silence and Creative Sound Play are so beneficial for children. These 12 Sound Activities are detailed in Chapter 14.

One of the indicators of achieving mastery is when adding variation and layering in levels of complexity becomes easy, fun, and creative. The more facile you all become, the greater the level of complexity you can dial in, or the quicker you can move on to thoroughly learning a new Sound Activity.

As you experience your first year with Creative Sound Play with your students, you will see how each of the three phases builds upon the one preceding. As you gain familiarity and confidence with working with Creative Sound Play, sound and silence will take on a whole new dimension. The more regularly and consistently you work with sound and silence on a daily basis, the more your children and classroom community will come together and resemble a well-oiled machine, and wonderful working ensemble.

19

Overview of the School Year

There are three phases of Creative Sound Play over the school year:

Phase I—(September, October, November, December)

Transform Transition Times into Short, Fun Learning Bursts Using the Quick Start Guide
- Develop and master three Primary Elements of Sound: pitch, volume, and duration using these four tried-and-true flexible transition activities:
- Quick Focus Warm-Up
- Fun with Counting
- All Aboard
- Sing with Purpose

Phase II—(January, February, March, April)

- Continue to use sound for transition times as part of your daily routine
- Begin to learn more of the 12 Sound Activities and include them in your transitions

As you and your students develop more control and facility with sound-making, the next level is to plan to schedule an additional 30–40 minutes a few days a week to include regular practice time using and playing a variety of handheld percussion instruments aka sound makers: drums, hand drums, shakers, cymbals, finger cymbals, triangles, tambourines, wood blocks, guiros, bells, hand bells, cowbells, claves, and maracas—in all the ways, everyone is mastering making sound.

Here is a recap of the 12 Sound Activities:

1. Counting, Clapping, and Stomping
2. Technique and Texture
3. Dynamic Control
4. Emphasis, Duration, and Pitch
5. Time and Tempo
6. Passing a Clap One-to-One
7. Dividing the Class into Groups
8. Improvising and Creating Dialogue
9. Rhythmic Literacy
10. Art Sounds
11. Conducting through Patterns
12. Conducting through Gesture

Phase III—Sound Sculpturing—(May and June)

Creating Sound Sculptures for Public Performance
- ♦ Compose, conduct, and perform Sound Sculptures: utilizing the Primary Elements of Sound and the 12 Sound Activities as the basis for creating Sound Sculptures and/or sound compositions that have a beginning, middle, and end, and that can be performed publicly.

20
Year-at-a-Glance by Month

Phase I—(September, October, November, December)
Transform Transition Times Into Short, Fun Learning Bursts using the Quick Start Guide

- Develop and master three Primary Elements of Sound: pitch, volume, and duration using these four tried-and-true flexible transition activities:
  - Quick Focus Warm-Up
  - Fun with Counting
  - All Aboard
  - Sing with Purpose

Phase II—(January, February, March, April)

- Continue to use sound for transition times as part of your daily routine
- Begin to learn more of the 12 Sound Activities and include them in your transitions
- As you and your students develop more control and facility with sound-making, the next level is to plan to schedule an additional 30–40 minutes a few days a week to include regular practice time using and playing a variety of handheld instruments

January
- ♦ Technique and Texture
- ♦ Emphasis, Duration, and Pitch
- ♦ Time and Tempo

February
1. Passing a Clap One-to-One
2. Dividing the Class into Groups
3. Improvising and Creating Dialogue

March
1. Rhythmic Literacy
2. Art Sounds

April
1. Conducting through Patterns
2. Conducting through Gesture

Phase III—Sound Sculpturing—(May and June)—creating Sound Sculptures for Public Performance

May and June
- ♦ Compose, conduct, and perform Sound Sculptures: utilizing the Primary Elements of Sound and the 12 Sound Activities as the basis for creating sound sculptures and/or sound compositions that have a beginning, middle, and end, and that can be performed publicly.

Sound Sculpturing—Creating and Presenting Sound Sculptures in Public Performance

21
The Weekly Schedule for Learning the 12 Sound Activities

Working with the Weekly Schedule

Please keep in mind that what follows in the weekly schedule are basic suggestions as to how to begin to approach working with the 12 Sound Activities. These steps are designed to help you and your class master each of the 12 Sound Activities as quickly and efficiently as possible.

Although the schedule shows that you are to work with one of the 12 Sound Activities per week, in reality, that is nothing less than a Herculean task and *not* meant to be done.

The *sole* reason I have written the schedule this way is to give you an idea of what kinds of possibilities, layers of complexity, and additional challenges are available to you once you and your students begin to gain mastery of deliberate and intentional sound-making.

It's not how many Sound Activities you work with that make the difference but how thoroughly and masterfully you and your students become in making intentional sound in deliberate ways based on the Sound Activity you are working with at any given time.

Depending on the age and sophistication of your students and the specific Sound Activity you are working on, you may choose to work with it for one, two, or three weeks, perhaps even

DOI: 10.4324/9781032636986-26

a month or more, in order to incorporate several added elements of complexity, including having your students take over and lead the Sound Activity.

In summary, working with Sound Activities on a consistent daily basis several times a day and scaffolding added complexity will keep the process fun and challenging while developing mastery and control.

Week 1—Counting, Clapping, and Stomping

Counting, clapping, and stomping mean gaining the ability to count and perform a deliberately controlled clap, stomp, or both on a given beat.

> In Practice—Monday Morning 9:30 A.M.
> Quick Focus Warm-Up—15 to 45 seconds
> Sound Activity—Counting, Clapping, and Stomping

Without any verbal instruction to your class, begin to count out loud at a moderate volume: 1, 2, 3, 4, 1, 2, 3, 4, 1, 2, 3, 4, etc.

Once everyone has caught on and is counting with you at a moderate volume, change it to a whisper. Once everyone is counting in a whisper, change it to a moderate volume. Once they are counting at a moderate level, change it to a loud volume. Once that is achieved, change it back to a moderate volume.

Now, continuing to count at a steady tempo 1, 2, 3, 4, 1, 2, 3, 4, etc., at a moderate volume, clap your hands only once every time you say the number 1.

Make sure you keep a steady tempo. Do this for as long as it takes for everyone to master counting 1, 2, 3, 4, 1, 2, 3, 4, etc., while clapping once every time the number 1 is said and counted out loud.

> In Practice—Monday 12 Noon
> Quick Focus Warm-Up—15 to 45 seconds
> Sound Activity—Counting, Clapping, and Stomping

Without any verbal instruction to your class, begin to count out loud at a moderate volume: 1, 2, 3, 4, 1, 2, 3, 4, 1, 2, 3, 4, etc.

Once everyone has caught on and is counting with you at a moderate volume, change it to a whisper. Once everyone is counting in a whisper, change it to a moderate volume. Once they are counting at a moderate level, change it to a loud volume. Once that is achieved, change it back to a moderate volume.

Now, continuing to count 1, 2, 3, 4, 1, 2, 3, 4, etc., at a moderate volume, clap your hands once every time you say the number 1.

Make sure you keep a steady tempo. Do this for as long as it takes for everyone to master counting 1, 2, 3, 4, 1, 2, 3, 4, etc., while clapping once every time the number 1 is said and counted out loud.

In Practice—Monday 2 P.M.
Quick Focus Warm-Up—15 to 45 seconds
Sound Activity—Counting, Clapping, and Stomping

Without any verbal instruction to your class, begin to count out loud at a moderate volume: 1, 2, 3, 4, 1, 2, 3, 4, 1, 2, 3, 4, etc.

Once everyone has caught on and is counting with you at a moderate volume, change it to a whisper. Once everyone is counting in a whisper, change it to a moderate volume. Once they are counting at a moderate level, change it to a loud volume. Once that is achieved, change it back to a moderate volume.

Now, continuing to count 1, 2, 3, 4, 1, 2, 3, 4, etc., at a moderate volume, clap your hands once every time you say the number 1.

Make sure you keep a steady tempo. Do this for as long as it takes for everyone to master counting 1, 2, 3, 4, 1, 2, 3, 4, etc., while clapping once every time the number 1 is said and counted out loud.

In Practice—Tuesday Morning 9:30 A.M.
Quick Focus Warm-Up—15–45 seconds
Sound Activity—Counting, Clapping, and Stomping
Adding Complexity—Make sure you keep a steady tempo, counting 1, 2, 3, 4, 1, 2, 3, 4, etc., at a moderate volume, but softly clap once when saying the number 2.

In Practice—Tuesday 12 Noon
Quick Focus Warm-Up—15–45 seconds
Sound Activity—Counting, Clapping, and Stomping
Adding Complexity—Make sure you keep a steady tempo, counting 1, 2, 3, 4, 1, 2, 3, 4, etc., at a soft volume, and loudly clap once when saying the number 2.

In Practice—Tuesday 2 P.M.
Quick Focus Warm-Up—15 to 45 seconds
Sound Activity—Counting, Clapping, and Stomping
Adding Complexity—Make sure you keep a steady tempo, counting 1, 2, 3, 4, 1, 2, 3, 4, etc., at a loud volume, and moderately clap once when saying the number 2.

In Practice—Wednesday Morning 9:30 A.M.
Quick Focus Warm-Up—15 to 45 seconds
Sound Activity—Counting, Clapping, and Stomping
Adding Complexity—Make sure you keep a steady tempo, counting 1, 2, 3, 4, 1, 2, 3, 4, etc., but stomp your right foot on 1 and pat your left shoulder when saying the number 3 and bark on the number 4.

In Practice—Wednesday 12 Noon
Quick Focus Warm-Up—15 to 45 seconds
Sound Activity—Counting, Clapping, and Stomping
Adding Complexity—Make sure you keep a steady tempo: counting 1, 2, 3, 4, 1, 2, 3, 4, etc., but now clap on 2 softly, quack on 3, and stomp your right foot on 4.

In Practice—Wednesday 2 P.M.
Quick Focus Warm-Up—15 to 45 seconds
Sound Activity: Counting, Clapping, and Stomping
Adding Complexity—Make sure you keep a steady tempo: counting 1, 2, 3, 4, 1, 2, 3, 4, etc., and say one in a whisper and only clap on the number 4.

In Practice—Thursday Morning 9:30 A.M.
Quick Focus Warm-Up—15 to 45 seconds
Sound Activity—Counting, Clapping, and Stomping

Adding Complexity—Make sure you keep a steady tempo, counting 1, 2, 3, 4, 1, 2, 3, 4, etc. Count every number in a whisper and clap loudly on 3.

In Practice—Thursday 12 Noon
Quick Focus Warm-Up—15 to 45 seconds
Sound Activity—Counting, Clapping, and Stomping
Adding Complexity—Make sure you keep a steady tempo, counting 1, 2, 3, 4, 1, 2, 3, 4, etc. Count every number in a moderately loud voice and clap very softly on 1.

In Practice—Thursday 2 P.M.
Quick Focus Warm-Up—15 to 45 seconds
Sound Activity—Counting, Clapping, and Stomping
Adding Complexity—Make sure you keep a steady tempo, counting 1, 2, 3, 4, 1, 2, 3, 4, etc. Clap on 1 and 3 and stomp on 4.

In Practice—Friday Morning 9:30 A.M.
Quick Focus Warm-Up—15 to 45 seconds
Sound Activity—Counting, Clapping, and Stomping
Adding Complexity—Make sure you keep a steady tempo, counting 1, 2, 3, 4, 1, 2, 3, 4, etc. Whisper on one, clap on 2, moo on 3, and stomp on 4.

In Practice—Friday 12 Noon
Quick Focus Warm-Up—15 to 45 seconds
Sound Activity—Counting, Clapping, and Stomping
Adding Complexity—Make sure you keep a steady tempo, counting 1, 2, 3, 4, 1, 2, 3, 4, etc. Clap on 1, stomp on 3, and speak loudly on 4.

In Practice—Friday 2 P.M.
Quick Focus Warm-Up—15 to 45 seconds
Sound Activity—Counting, Clapping, and Stomping
Adding Complexity—Make sure you keep a steady tempo, counting 1, 2, 3, 4, 1, 2, 3, 4, etc. Ask the students how they want to add complexity to the exercise. Have one of your students lead it.

Depending on you, your class, and how fast everyone picks this up, feel free to add more and more complexity. Change the number count from 1 to 4 but now from 1 to 3, 1 to 5, 1 to 6, and so on. Count backward. Clap loudly on 1, stomp softly on 2, speak loudly on 3, and whisper on 4. Add animal sounds, clap medium on 1, bark loudly on 2, silence on 3, and stomp your right foot on 4. Most importantly, always have fun with sound and use your imagination! And don't forget to let your students decide what sounds to use as well as to lead the class.

Week 2—Technique and Texture

Technique and texture mean developing the controlled ability to deliberately create sounds that produce different types of textures. For now, we will only use our hands to generate sound.

There are four basic ways to clap hands. Each makes a different kind of clap sound and texture. There are two basic ways to rub hands.

<u>The Four Ways to Clap</u>:
Flat Clap: This is when both hands are flat, resembling praying hands. This type of clap produces a relatively crisp sound without much resonance.
Monster Clap: This is where both hands are at right angles to each other (or cross), are cupped, and create an air pocket that when clapped creates a more hollow, resonant, deep sound.
Applause Clap: This is similar to the monster clap, as both hands are at right angles to each other. But the fingers are closed and strike the palm of the other hand. This type of clap allows for the greatest range of volume, from soft to loud, while still maintaining a rich resonant sound.
Pat Clap: This is where one hand gently pats the other hand; it tends to make the lightest, softest sound of the four types of claps.

<u>Rubbing Hands:</u>
Back-and-Forth Rub: This produces a two-stroke sound. You can do this with just hands or hands that rub arms, legs, etc.

Round Rub: This creates a circular sound that seems to go on forever. One can do this with just hands or hands that rub arms, tummies, legs, etc.

In Practice—Monday 9:30 A.M.
Quick Focus Warm-Up—15 to 45 seconds
Sound Activity—Technique and Texture

Demonstrate to the class the four ways of clapping and have everyone investigate the types of sounds.

In Practice—Monday 12 Noon
Quick Focus Warm-Up—15 to 45 seconds
Sound Activity—Technique and Texture

Continue exploring the four different ways to clap.

In Practice—Monday 2 P.M.
Quick Focus Warm-Up—15 to 45 seconds
Sound Activity—Technique and Texture

Continue exploring the four different ways to clap.

In Practice—Tuesday Morning 9:30 A.M.
Quick Focus Warm-Up—15 to 45 seconds
Sound Activity—Technique and Texture

Continue exploring the four different ways to clap.

In Practice—Tuesday 12 Noon
Quick Focus Warm-Up—15 to 45 seconds
Sound Activity—Technique and Texture

Ask your students to demonstrate the different ways to clap and rub hands.

In Practice—Tuesday 2 P.M.
Quick Focus Warm-Up—15 to 45 seconds
Sound Activity—Technique and Texture

Ask your students to demonstrate the different ways to clap and rub hands.

> In Practice—Wednesday 9:30 A.M.
> Quick Focus Warm-Up—15 to 45 seconds
> Sound Activity—Technique and Texture

Count 1, 2, 3, 4, 1, 2, 3, 4, etc., and play a monster clap on 1 and a flat cap on 3.

> In Practice—Wednesday 12 Noon
> Quick Focus Warm-Up—15 to 45 seconds
> Sound Activity—Technique and Texture

Count 1, 2, 3, 4, 1, 2, 3, 4, etc., and play a monster clap on 2 and a flat clap on 4.

> In Practice—Wednesday 2 P.M.
> Quick Focus Warm-Up—15 to 45 seconds
> Sound Activity—Technique and Texture

Count 1, 2, 3, 4, 1, 2, 3, 4, etc., and play an applause clap on 1 and a pat clap on 3.

> In Practice—Thursday Morning 9:30 A.M.
> Quick Focus Warm-Up—15 to 45 seconds
> Sound Activity—Technique and Texture

Count 1, 2, 3, 4, 1, 2, 3, 4, etc., and play a flat clap on 1, a monster clap on 2, a flat clap on 3, and a monster clap on 4.

> In Practice—Thursday 12 Noon
> Quick Focus Warm-Up—15 to 45 seconds
> Sound Activity—Technique and Texture

Count 1, 2, 3, 4, 1, 2, 3, 4. For the full count of 4 beats (1, 2, 3, 4), play the round rub followed by four pat claps on every beat (1, 2, 3, 4).

In Practice—Thursday 2 P.M.
Quick Focus Warm-Up—15 to 45 seconds
Sound Activity—Technique and Texture

Count 1, 2, 3, 4, 1, 2, 3, 4. Play the applause clap on every beat, but this time, switch the hand that is striking the other hand. For right-handed people, the left hand should strike the right hand; for left-handed people, the right hand should strike the left.

In Practice—Friday Morning 9:30 A.M.
Quick Focus Warm-Up—15 to 45 seconds
Sound Activity—Technique and Texture

Ask your students which claps they want to play and how. Have a student lead it.

In Practice—Friday 12 Noon
Quick Focus Warm-Up—15 to 45 seconds
Sound Activity—Technique and Texture

Ask your students which claps they want to play and how. Have a student lead it.

In Practice—Friday 2 P.M.
Quick Focus Warm-Up—15 to 45 seconds
Sound Activity—Technique and Texture

Ask your students which claps they want to play and how. Have a student lead it.

Week 3—Dynamic Control
This is the ability to create controlled sound at variable levels of volume: quiet, medium, and loud, and everything in between.

In Practice—Monday 9:30 A.M.
Quick Focus Warm-Up—15 to 45 seconds
Sound Activity—Dynamic Control

Count 1, 2, 3, 1, 2, 3, 1, 2, 3, and repeat counting for 20 to 30 seconds. Play every beat with an applause clap. Start very softly and gradually get louder and louder. This exercise should take at least 20 to 30 seconds to go from the softest clap to the loudest clap.

In Practice—Monday 12 Noon
Quick Focus Warm-Up—15 to 45 seconds
Sound Activity—Dynamic Control

Count 1, 2, 3, 1, 2, 3, 1, 2, 3, and repeat counting for 20 to 30 seconds. Play every beat with an applause clap. Start quiet and gradually get louder and louder. This exercise should take at least 20 to 30 seconds to go from the quietest clap to the loudest clap.

In Practice—Monday 2 P.M.
Quick Focus Warm-Up—15 to 45 seconds
Sound Activity—Dynamic Control

Count 1, 2, 3, 4, 1, 2, 3, 4. Play every beat with an applause clap, start very loudly then gradually get quieter and quieter. This exercise should take at least 20 to 30 seconds to go from the loudest clap to the softest clap.

In Practice—Tuesday Morning 9:30 A.M.
Quick Focus Warm-Up—15 to 45 seconds
Sound Activity—Dynamic Control

Introduce three different levels of volume: quiet, medium, and loud. To indicate quiet, your arm should fully extend down. To indicate medium, your arm should be at chest level. To indicate loud, your arm should be extended upward at head level. Now, have your students clap freely (not in any tempo per se) but at the desired volume level you conduct and indicate.

In Practice—Tuesday 12 Noon
Quick Focus Warm-Up—15 to 45 seconds
Sound Activity—Dynamic Control

Introduce three different levels of volume: soft, medium, and loud. To indicate soft, your arm should fully extend down. To indicate medium, your arm should be at chest level. To indicate loud, your arm should be extended upward at head level. Now, have your students clap freely (not in any tempo per se) at the desired volume level you conduct and indicate.

In Practice—Tuesday 2 P.M.
Quick Focus Warm-Up—15 to 45 seconds
Sound Activity—Dynamic Control

Invite students to conduct the three different levels of volume.

In Practice—Wednesday Morning 9:30 A.M.
Quick Focus Warm-Up—15 to 45 seconds
Sound Activity—Dynamic Control

Slowly count out loud 1, 2, 3, 4, 1, 2, 3, 4, and have everyone play a monster clap on every beat. Conduct different levels of volume with your hand. Move it around—don't just go from quiet to loud and loud to quiet. Mix it up. Go from quiet to medium, to quiet, to loud, to medium, to loud, and back to quiet.

In Practice—Wednesday 12 Noon
Quick Focus Warm-Up—15 to 45 seconds
Sound Activity—Dynamic Control

Slowly count out loud 1, 2, 3, 4, 1, 2, 3, 4, and have everyone play a monster clap on every beat. Conduct different levels of volume with your hand. Move it around—don't just go from quiet to loud and loud to quiet. Mix it up. Go from quiet to medium, to quiet, to loud, to medium, to loud, and back to quiet.

In Practice—Wednesday 2 P.M.
Quick Focus Warm-Up—15 to 45 seconds
Sound Activity—Dynamic Control

Slowly count out loud 1, 2, 3, 4, 1, 2, 3, 4, and have everyone play a monster clap on every beat. Conduct different levels of volume with your hand. Move it around—don't just go from quiet to loud and loud to quiet. Mix it up. Go from quiet to medium, to quiet, to loud, to medium, to loud, and back to quiet.

In Practice—Thursday Morning 9:30 A.M.
Quick Focus Warm-Up—15 to 45 seconds
Sound Activity—Dynamic Control

Slowly count out loud 1, 2, 3, 4, 1, 2, 3, 4, etc. For each count of four beats, gradually change the level of volume. Start out at a medium volume and get quieter for four beats. Over the next four beats, gradually get louder and return to a medium volume, and continue over the next four beats to a loud volume. Over the next four beats, return to a medium volume.

In Practice—Thursday 12 Noon
Quick Focus Warm-Up—15 to 45 seconds
Sound Activity—Dynamic Control

Slowly count out loud 1, 2, 3, 4, 1, 2, 3, 4, etc. For each count of four beats, gradually change the level of volume. Start out at a medium volume and get quieter for four beats.
 Over the next four beats, gradually get louder and return to a medium volume, and continue over the next four beats to a loud volume. Over the next four beats, return to a medium volume.

In Practice—Thursday 2 P.M.
Quick Focus Warm-Up—15 to 45 seconds
Sound Activity—Dynamic Control

Slowly count out loud 1, 2, 3, 4, 1, 2, 3, 4, etc. For each count of four beats, gradually change the level of volume. Start out at a medium volume and get quieter for four beats.
 Over the next four beats, gradually get louder and return to a medium volume, and continue over the next four beats to a loud volume. Over the next four beats, return to a medium volume.

In Practice—Friday Morning 9:30 A.M.
Quick Focus Warm-Up—15 to 45 seconds
Sound Activity—Dynamic Control

Count 1, 2, 3, 4, 1, 2, 3, 4. Play every beat with an applause clap; start very loudly and then gradually get quieter and quieter. This exercise should take at least 20 to 30 seconds to go from the loudest clap to the softest clap.

In Practice—Friday 12 Noon
Quick Focus Warm-Up—15 to 45 seconds
Sound Activity—Dynamic Control

Invite students to decide and conduct how they want to create sound dynamically.

In Practice—Friday 2 P.M.
Quick Focus Warm-Up—15 to 45 seconds
Sound Activity—Dynamic Control

Invite students to decide and conduct how they want to create sound dynamically.

Week 4—Emphasis, Duration, and Pitch

This is the ability to deliberately control how a sound is made: short or long, loud, medium, or quiet. This resembles how people choose to accentuate and emphasize (or not emphasize) words, or parts of words and syllables, to convey meaning when they speak.

In Practice—Monday 9:30 A.M.
Quick Focus Warm-Up—15 to 45 seconds
Sound Activity—Emphasis, Duration, and Pitch

Slowly count out loud 1, 2, 3, 4, 1, 2, 3, 4, and repeat. Make sure the sounds of the numbers are long in length and seem connected to when the next number begins and are at a medium or moderate volume level.

Now, slowly count again at the same speed and punctuate (emphasize) every number but as short as you can. Make sure your students are punctuating each number and that they are not connected to each other. Make sure that there is silence surrounding each number. This is to be done at a moderate volume—*not* loud.

As you count and repeat the numbers 1, 2, 3, 4, sound out the first group as long connected sounds, and then as you count the second group of numbers at the same tempo, sound them out as short sounds with silence in between each number.

In Practice—Monday 12 Noon
Quick Focus Warm-Up—15 to 45 seconds
Sound Activity—Emphasis, Duration, and Pitch

Slowly count out loud 1, 2, 3, 4, 1, 2, 3, 4, etc.

Slowly count out loud 1, 2, 3, 4, 1, 2, 3, 4, and repeat. Make sure the sounds of the numbers are long in length and seem connected to when the next number begins and are at a medium or moderate volume level.

Now, slowly count again at the same speed and punctuate (emphasize) every number but as short as you can. Make sure your students are punctuating each number and that they are not connected to each other. Make sure that there is silence surrounding each number. This is to be done at a moderate volume—*not* loud.

As you count and repeat the numbers 1, 2, 3, 4, sound out the first group as long connected sounds, and then as you count the second group of numbers, sound them out as short sounds with silence in between each number.

In Practice—Monday 2 P.M.
Quick Focus Warm-Up—15 to 45 seconds
Sound Activity—Emphasis, Duration, and Pitch

Slowly count out loud 1, 2, 3, 4, 1, 2, 3, 4, and repeat. Make sure the sounds of the numbers are long in length and seem connected to when the next number begins and are at a medium or moderate volume level.

Now, slowly count again at the same speed and punctuate (emphasize) every number but as short as you can. Make sure your students are punctuating each number and that they are not connected to each other. Make sure that there is silence surrounding each number. This is to be done at a moderate volume—*not* loud.

As you count and repeat the numbers 1, 2, 3, 4, sound out the first group as long connected sounds, and then as you count the second group of numbers, sound them out as short sounds with silence in between each number.

In Practice—Tuesday Morning 9:30 A.M.
Quick Focus Warm-Up—15 to 45 seconds
Sound Activity—Emphasis, Duration, and Pitch

Slowly count out loud 1, 2, 3, 4, 1, 2, 3, 4, etc.

Make sure all of the sounds of the numbers are long in length and connect to the next number.

Now, when saying only the number 3, make the pitch high (squeaky), and make sure it is at the same volume as all of the numbers.

Once your students are following you and making a squeaky sound for the number 3, make the length of only the squeaky number 3 sound very short, followed by a little silence. All of the other numbers, 1, 2, and 4, should remain long in length and at the same volume level as when you began.

You are accenting the number three and adding a short articulation.

In Practice—Tuesday 12 Noon
Quick Focus Warm-Up—15 to 45 seconds
Sound Activity—Emphasis, Duration, and Pitch

Slowly count out loud 1, 2, 3, 4, 1, 2, 3, 4, etc.

Make sure all of the sounds of the numbers are long in length and connect to the next number.

Now, when saying only the number 3, make the pitch high (squeaky), but make sure it is at the same volume as all of the numbers.

Once your students are following you and making a squeaky sound for the number 3, make the length of only the squeaky number 3 sound very short, followed by a little silence. All of the other numbers, 1, 2, and 4, should remain long in length and at the same volume level as when you began.

You are accenting the number three and adding a short articulation.

In Practice—Tuesday 2 P.M.
Quick Focus Warm-Up—15 to 45 seconds
Sound Activity—Emphasis, Duration, and Pitch

Slowly count out loud 1, 2, 3, 4, 1, 2, 3, 4, etc.

Make sure all of the sounds of the numbers are long in length and connect to the next number.

Now, when saying only the number 3, make the pitch high (squeaky), but make sure it is at the same volume as all of the numbers.

Once your students are following you and making a squeaky sound for the number 3, make the length of only the squeaky number 3 sound very short, followed by a little silence. All of the other numbers, 1, 2, and 4, should remain long in length and at the same volume level as when you began.

You are accenting the number three and adding a short articulation.

In Practice—Wednesday Morning 9:30 A.M.
Quick Focus Warm-Up—15 to 45 seconds
Sound Activity—Emphasis, Duration, and Pitch

Slowly count out at a medium volume 1, 2, 3, 4, 1, 2, 3, 4, etc.

Add a monster clap on number 1. Sound out 2 long, sound out 3 short and high in pitch, and stomp your left foot on 4.

In Practice—Wednesday 12 Noon
Quick Focus Warm-Up—15 to 45 seconds
Sound Activity—Emphasis, Duration, and Pitch

Slowly count out at a medium volume 1, 2, 3, 4, 1, 2, 3, 4, etc.
Add a monster clap on number 1. Sound out 2 long, sound out 3 short and high in pitch, and stomp your left foot on 4.

In Practice—Wednesday 2 P.M.
Quick Focus Warm-Up—15 to 45 seconds
Sound Activity—Emphasis, Duration, and Pitch

Slowly count out at a medium volume 1, 2, 3, 4, 1, 2, 3, 4, etc.
Add a monster clap on number 1. Sound out 2 long, sound out 3 short, and high in pitch, and stomp your left foot on 4.

In Practice—Thursday Morning 9:30 A.M.
Quick Focus Warm-Up—15 to 45 seconds
Sound Activity—Emphasis, Duration, and Pitch

Slowly count in a whisper 1, 2, 3, 4, 1, 2, 3, 4, and repeat.
Sound out 1 short, 2 high in pitch and long, stomp on 3, and do a flat clap on 4.

In Practice—Thursday 12 Noon
Quick Focus Warm-Up—15 to 45 seconds
Sound Activity—Emphasis, Duration, and Pitch

Slowly count in a whisper 1, 2, 3, 4, 1, 2, 3, 4, and repeat.
Sound 1 short, 2 high in pitch and long, stomp on 3, and do a flat clap on 4.

In Practice—Thursday 2 P.M.
Quick Focus Warm-Up—15 to 45 seconds
Sound Activity—Emphasis, Duration, and Pitch

Slowly count in a whisper 1, 2, 3, 4, 1, 2, 3, 4, and repeat.
Sound 1 short, 2 high in pitch and long, stomp on 3, and do a flat clap on 4.

In Practice—Friday Morning 9:30 A.M.
Quick Focus Warm-Up—15 to 45 seconds
Sound Activity—Emphasis, Duration, and Pitch

Invite the class to decide what numbers (beats) to accent, which sounds they want to use for each beat, which ones they want to play short or long, and at what volume they want to perform it. This pattern should be noted and practiced for the rest of the day.

In Practice—Friday 12 Noon
Quick Focus Warm-Up—15 to 45 seconds
Sound Activity—Emphasis, Duration, and Pitch

Invite the class to decide what numbers (beats) to accent, which sounds they want to use for each beat, which ones they want to play short or long, and at what volume they want to perform it. This pattern should be noted and practiced for the rest of the day.

In Practice—Friday 2 P.M.
Quick Focus Warm-Up—15 to 45 seconds
Sound Activity—Emphasis, Duration, and Pitch

Invite the class to decide what numbers (beats) to accent, which sounds they want to use for each beat, which ones they want to play short or long, and at what volume they want to perform it. This pattern should be noted and practiced for the rest of the day.

Now that you have a fundamental idea of Emphasis, Duration and Pitch experiment with sounding out letters, syllables, words and sentences in all kinds of different ways that help to convey the meaning, and emotional sentiment of what we are expressing.

Week 5—Time and Tempo

This may be the most complex Sound Activity to execute, not because it's difficult, but because it's probably the one most associated with "music." Because of this, I am simply going to repeat here in the weekly schedule again how you can learn the ability to control and keep a steady tempo.

This is a matter of simply understanding how sounds and silences interact in time. For all of you who feel you have no rhythm, that is false. We all have hearts; they beat in "rhythm" or time, and the heart is the first drum.

So for keeping a steady tempo, can you count for the duration of one second? Of course, you can: say out loud 1 potato. That is about the same length as one second of sound. Now say 1 potato, 2 potato, and you have now just counted the equivalent of how long two seconds last.

Now, simply count 1 potato, 2 potato, 3 potato, 4 potato and clap your hands every time you say the number. This is a steady tempo and is roughly one beat per second. Repeat this slowly a few times and get comfortable. There is no rush nor any judgment. Everyone is completely capable of this, and the more you practice this with your students, the easier it will become. And don't forget, your students will love it. Just think of all the complex words that have several syllables you can use to practice with: 1 banana, 2 banana, 3 banana, 4 banana…1 papaya, 2 papaya, 3 papaya, 4 papaya. And to make the tempo even a little slower, add more syllables—1 pepperoni pizza, 2 peperoni pizza, 3 pepperoni pizza, and so on.

And for faster tempos that you want to keep constant, just count fewer syllables. For example, repeat what we just did earlier and count at the same speed, clapping only when you say the number—1 potato, 2 potato, 3 potato, 4 potato. Now, keep counting at the same speed, but just count 1 po, 2 po, 3 po, 4 po, and clap on every number. Presto you have a constant tempo that is just about twice as fast as the one when counting 1 potato, 2 potato, 3 potato, 4 potato. It's all about the amount of syllables you count.

So now let's have a blast going between the potato and po, clapping only on the numbers—1 potato, 2 potato, 1 po, 2 po, 3 po, 4 po, 1 potato, 2 potato, 1 po, 2 po, 3 po, 4 po.

And finally, once you have mastered counting the numbers and syllables out loud at a slow tempo while you clap on a given number or syllable, switch it up and count the numbers and syllables but now only in your head. You can continue to move your lips, bob your head, and even tap your foot lightly as you count only in your head, just don't make any sound. Then clap your hands on a given number or syllable and hear how steady your clapping sound is. Who says you don't have rhythm?

In Practice—Monday 9:30 A.M.
Quick Focus Warm-Up—15 to 45 seconds
Sound Activity—Time and Tempo

With your class, count to yourself—*not* out loud—and clap. Have your students close their eyes, listen to you clap, and try to clap in sync with you. As your students clap with you, try to listen to the space in between the clapping sound and focus on the silence between claps. Listen to how even and regular you and your students can make the space in between your claps last. Do this several times.

In Practice—Monday 12 Noon
Quick Focus Warm-Up—15 to 45 seconds
Sound Activity—Time and Tempo

With your class, count to yourself—*not* out loud—and clap. Have your students close their eyes, listen to you clap, and try to clap in sync with you. As your students clap with you, try to listen to the space in between the clapping sound and focus on the silence between claps. Listen to how even and regular you and your students can make the space in between your claps last. Do this several times.

In Practice—Monday 2 P.M.
Quick Focus Warm-Up—15 to 45 seconds
Sound Activity—Time and Tempo

With your class, count to yourself—*not* out loud—and clap. Have your students close their eyes, listen to you clap, and try to clap in sync with you. As your students clap with you, try to listen to the space in between the clapping sound and focus on the silence between claps. Listen to how even and regular you and your students can make the space in between your claps last. Do this several times.

In Practice—Tuesday Morning 9:30 A.M.
Quick Focus Warm-Up—15 to 45 seconds
Sound Activity—Time and Tempo

Count to yourself—*not* out loud—and clap. Have your students close their eyes, listen, and try to clap in sync with you. As everyone is playing at the same tempo, slowly, gradually, and deliberately begin to speed up the tempo. As you do so, be aware that as it begins to speed up, you may lose control of your class, and they may increase the speed faster than you intend. Do your best to hold it down. DO NOT GO WITH THE CLASS. Stop the class and begin again at the original slow tempo when that happens. Do this a few times. Note: this exercise is about enhancing sensitivity and active listening skills. It is also important that the volume stay the same and not get louder as the tempos speed up.

In Practice—Tuesday 12 Noon
Quick Focus Warm-Up—15 to 45 seconds
Sound Activity—Time and Tempo

Count to yourself—*not* out loud—and clap. Have your students close their eyes, listen, and try to clap in sync with you. As everyone is playing at the same tempo, slowly, gradually, and deliberately begin to speed up the tempo. As you do so, be aware that as it begins to speed up, you may lose control of your class, and they may increase the speed faster than you intend. Do your best to hold it down. DO NOT GO WITH THE CLASS. Stop the class and begin again at the original slow tempo when that happens. Do this a few times. Note: this exercise is about enhancing sensitivity and active listening skills. It is also important that the volume stay the same and not get louder as the tempos speed up.

In Practice—Tuesday 2 P.M.
Quick Focus Warm-Up—15 to 45 seconds
Sound Activity—Time and Tempo

Count to yourself—*not* out loud—and clap. Have your students close their eyes, listen, and try to clap in sync with you.

As everyone is playing at the same tempo, slowly, gradually, and deliberately begin to speed up the tempo. As you do so, be aware that as it begins to speed up, you may lose control of your class, and they may increase the speed faster than you intend. Do your best to hold it down. DO NOT GO WITH THE CLASS. Stop the class and begin again at the original slow tempo when that happens. Do this a few times. Note: this exercise is about enhancing sensitivity and active listening skills. It is also important that the volume stay the same and not get louder as the tempos speed up.

In Practice—Wednesday Morning 9:30 A.M.
Quick Focus Warm-Up—15 to 45 seconds
Sound Activity—Time and Tempo

Have your students close their eyes, listen to you, and clap with you. Begin your clapping, but now at a notably faster tempo. Gradually and evenly, begin to slow the speed of the tempo down. Contrary to what happens when speeding up the tempo, people rarely speed up slowing down. Do this a few times.

In Practice—Wednesday 12 Noon
Quick Focus Warm-Up—15 to 45 seconds
Sound Activity—Time and Tempo

Have your students close their eyes, listen to you, and clap with you. Begin your clapping, but now at a notably faster tempo. Gradually and evenly, begin to slow the speed of the tempo down. Contrary to what happens when speeding up the tempo, people rarely speed up slowing down. Do this a few times.

In Practice—Wednesday 2 P.M.
Quick Focus Warm-Up—15 to 45 seconds
Sound Activity—Time and Tempo

Have your students close their eyes, listen to you, and clap with you. Begin your clapping, but now at a notably faster tempo. Gradually and evenly, begin to slow the speed of the tempo down. Contrary to what happens when speeding up the tempo, people rarely speed up slowing down. Do this a few times.

In Practice—Thursday Morning 9:30 A.M.
Quick Focus Warm-Up—15 to 45 seconds
Sound Activity—Time and Tempo

Have your students close their eyes, listen to you, and clap with you. Begin your clapping at a slow tempo: 1 potato, 2 potato, etc. Gradually and evenly, begin to speed up the tempo. Keep it steady for 10 seconds or so, then slow it down to the original tempo. Do this a few times.

In Practice—Thursday 12 Noon
Quick Focus Warm-Up—15 to 45 seconds
Sound Activity—Time and Tempo

Have your students close their eyes, listen to you, and clap with you. Begin your clapping at a slow tempo: 1 potato, 2 potato, etc. Gradually and evenly, begin to speed up the tempo. Keep it steady for 10 seconds or so, then slow it down to the original tempo. Do this a few times.

In Practice—Thursday 2 P.M.
Quick Focus Warm-Up—15 to 45 seconds
Sound Activity—Time and Tempo

Have your students close their eyes, listen to you, and clap with you. Start slowly. Quietly and gradually get faster, but make sure the volume does not get louder. In most situations, students get louder as the tempo speeds up. Pay close attention to this, and repeat this a few times.

In Practice—Friday Morning 9:30 A.M.
Quick Focus Warm-Up—15 to 45 seconds
Sound Activity—Time and Tempo

Have your students close their eyes, listen to you, and clap with you. Start slowly. Quietly and gradually get faster, but make sure the volume does not get louder. In most situations, students get louder as the tempo speeds up. Pay close attention to this, and repeat this a few times.

<u>Practice—Friday 12 Noon</u>
Quick Focus Warm-Up—15 to 45 seconds
Sound Activity—Time and Tempo

Have your students close their eyes, listen to you, and clap with you. Start at a fast tempo and at a quiet volume, and slowly and gradually slow down the tempo and get louder in volume. This is counterintuitive, so pay close attention. Repeat this a few times.

<u>In Practice—Friday 2 P.M.</u>
Quick Focus Warm-Up—15 to 45 seconds
Sound Activity—Time and Tempo

Have your students close their eyes, listen to you, and clap with you. Start at a fast tempo and at a quiet volume, then slowly and gradually decrease the tempo and get louder. This is counterintuitive, so pay close attention. Repeat this a few times.

Week 6—Passing a Clap One-to-One
This is the ability to move a sound from one person to another, one at a time. It is much like the game "telephone" that we played as kids, but here only with sound.

The other aspect to listen for is trying to make the amount of silence on either side of a clap even. Allow yourself to experiment with this without judgment. This is probably the most zen aspect of sound because it's all about trusting the silence. From my experience, most people clap and then shortchange the silence and rush to make the next clap. Try not to shortchange the silence, which is just as important if not more important than the clap sound. Silence allows for a pause and a breadth and defines the space around the sound. Just listen for it and trust that you will hear it.

<u>In Practice—Monday 9:30 A.M.</u>
Quick Focus Warm-Up—15 to 45 seconds
Sound Activity— Passing a Clap One-to-One

To begin, single out one student to play with. Face your student and clap once. When they respond with one clap, respond with one clap. Go back and forth several times, passing one clap to each other at a slow to moderate tempo. Listen to the silent space in between each clap and try to make sure that the tempo doesn't speed up or slow down. Do this with several students.

> In Practice—Monday 12 Noon
> Quick Focus Warm-Up—15 to 45 seconds
> Sound Activity—Passing a Clap One-to-One

Continue passing a clap back and forth with other students.

> In Practice—Monday 2 P.M.
> Quick Focus Warm-Up—15 to 45 seconds
> Sound Activity—Passing a Clap One-to-One

Continue passing a clap back and forth with other students until all of them have had a chance.

> In Practice—Tuesday Morning 9:30 A.M.
> Quick Focus Warm-Up—15 to 45 seconds
> Sound Activity—Passing a Clap One-to-One

Divide the class into pairs and have them pass a clap to each other.

> In Practice—Tuesday 12 Noon
> Quick Focus Warm-Up—15 to 45 seconds
> Sound Activity—Passing a Clap One-to-One

Divide the class into pairs and have them pass a clap to each other.

> In Practice—Tuesday 2 P.M.
> Quick Focus Warm-Up—15 to 45 seconds
> Sound Activity—Passing a Clap One-to-One

Divide the class into pairs and have them pass a clap to each other.

In Practice—Wednesday Morning 9:30 A.M.
Quick Focus Warm-Up—15 to 45 seconds
Sound Activity—Passing a Clap One-to-One

Divide the class into groups of three and have them pass a clap to each other at a slow to moderate tempo. Make sure everyone is listening to the silent space in between each clap, and try to make sure that the tempo doesn't speed up or slow down.

In Practice—Wednesday 12 Noon
Quick Focus Warm-Up—15 to 45 seconds
Sound Activity—Passing a Clap One-to-One

Divide the class into groups of four and have them pass a clap to each other at a slow to moderate tempo. Make sure everyone is listening to the silent space in between each clap, and try to make sure that the tempo doesn't speed up or slow down.

In Practice—Wednesday 2 P.M.
Quick Focus Warm-Up—15 to 45 seconds
Sound Activity—Passing a Clap One-to-One

Divide the class into groups of five and have them pass a clap to each other at a slow to moderate tempo. Make sure everyone is listening to the silent space in between each clap, and try to make sure that the tempo doesn't speed up or slow down.

In Practice—Thursday Morning 9:30 A.M.
Quick Focus Warm-Up—15 to 45 seconds
Sound Activity—Passing a Clap One-to-One

Have the class stand or sit in a full circle, count at a moderate tempo, and pass the clap around the room. Change directions.

In Practice—Thursday 12 Noon
Quick Focus Warm-Up—15 to 45 seconds
Sound Activity—Passing a Clap One-to-One

Have the class stand or sit in a full circle, count at a moderate tempo, and pass the clap around the room. Change directions.

   In Practice—Thursday 2 P.M.
   Quick Focus Warm-Up—15 to 45 seconds
   Sound Activity—Passing a Clap One-to-One

Have the class stand or sit in a full circle, count a moderate tempo, and pass the clap around the room. Change directions.

   In Practice—Friday Morning 9:30 A.M.
   Quick Focus Warm-Up—15 to 45 seconds
   Sound Activity—Passing a Clap One-to-One

Have the class stand or sit in a full circle, close their eyes, count at a moderate tempo, and pass the clap around the room. Change directions.

   In Practice—Friday 12 Noon
   Quick Focus Warm-Up—15 to 45 seconds
   Sound Activity–Passing a Clap One-to-One

Have the class stand or sit in a full circle, close their eyes, count at a moderate tempo, and pass the clap around the room. Change directions.

   In Practice—Friday 2 P.M.
   Quick Focus Warm-Up—15 to 45 seconds
   Sound Activity—Passing a Clap One-to-One

Have the class stand or sit in a full circle, close their eyes, count at a moderate tempo, and pass the clap around the room. Change directions.

Week 7—Dividing the Class into Groups
This is about dividing the ensemble—or class—into smaller parts in order to achieve the goal of being able to create deliberately

organized types of sounds that can be played at any given time. This fosters the ability to generate more complexity when creating sound—i.e., adding counterpoint and different types of textures. You can have two, three, four, or more groups—Team A, Team B, Team C, Team D, etc.—playing different types of sounds or lines (elements) at the same time, creating a whole, much like an orchestra with its string, brass, woodwind, and percussion sections.

How to learn the different parts:

It's always best to have the class as a whole play, learn, and practice all of the individual parts together prior to dividing the class into teams. Once everyone can perform the individual parts together easily, it's time to divide the class into teams and have each team play their parts alone. It is very important that each team have the time necessary to play their part with confidence. During this time, it's very important that each team practice and play their parts alone while the other team waits quietly and listens. Once everyone is comfortable with their parts, it's time to put them together as a full ensemble. The last element is that all the teams should have the opportunity to play all the different parts.

In Practice—Monday 9:30 A.M.
Quick Focus Warm-Up—15 to 45 seconds
Sound Activity—Dividing the Class into Groups

Divide the class into two teams, A and B.
   Slowly count out loud 1, 2, 3, 4, 1, 2, 3, 4, etc.
   Team A plays one loud monster clap on the count of 1, while Team B plays a quiet pat clap on the count of 3.
   Then have Teams A and B switch their parts.

In Practice—Monday 12 Noon
Quick Focus Warm-Up—15 to 45 seconds
Sound Activity—Dividing the Class into Groups

Divide the class into two teams: A and B.
   Slowly count out loud: 1, 2, 3, 4, 1, 2, 3, 4, etc.

Team A plays a round rub on 1 and a short vocal accent on 3. Team B stomps on 2 and plays a flat clap on 4.
Then have Teams A and B switch their parts.

In Practice—Monday 2 P.M.
Quick Focus Warm-Up—15 to 45 seconds
Sound Activity—Dividing the Class into Groups

Divide the class into two teams: A and B.
Slowly count out loud 1, 2, 3, 4, 1, 2, 3, 4, etc.
Team A plays a round rub on 1 and a short vocal accent on 3. Team B stomps on 2 and plays a flat clap on 4.
Then have Teams A and B switch their parts.

In Practice—Tuesday Morning 9:30 A.M.
Quick Focus Warm-Up—15 to 45 seconds
Sound Activity—Dividing the Class into Groups

Divide the class into two teams, A and B.
Slowly count out loud 1, 2, 3, 4, 5, 6, 7, 8, 1, 2, 3, 4, 5, 6, 7, 8 and repeat.
Team A plays only the first four counts: 1, 2, 3, 4, playing an applause clap on every count that begins very quietly and over the 4 counts gets very loud with every clap.
Team B plays counts 5, 6, 7, 8, playing an applause clap that begins very loudly and gets very quiet with every clap.
Teams A and B should alternate.

In Practice—Tuesday 12 Noon
Quick Focus Warm-Up—15 to 45 seconds
Sound Activity—Dividing the Class into Groups

Divide the class into two teams, A and B.
Slowly count out loud 1, 2, 3, 4, 5, 6, 7, 8, 1, 2, 3, 4, 5, 6, 7, 8 and repeat.
Team A plays only the first four counts: 1, 2, 3, 4, playing an applause clap on every count that begins very quietly and over the 4 counts gets very loud with every clap.

Team B plays counts 5, 6, 7, 8, playing an applause clap that begins very loudly and gets very quiet with every clap.
Teams A and B should alternate.

<u>In Practice—Tuesday 2 P.M.</u>
Quick Focus Warm-Up—15 to 45 seconds
Sound Activity—Dividing the Class into Groups

Divide the class into two teams, A and B.
Slowly count out loud 1, 2, 3, 4, 5, 6, 7, 8, 1, 2, 3, 4, 5, 6, 7, 8 and repeat.
Team A plays only the first four counts: 1, 2, 3, 4, playing an applause clap on every count that begins very quietly and over the 4 counts gets very loud with every clap.
Team B plays counts 5, 6, 7, 8, playing an applause clap that begins very loudly and gets very quiet with every clap.
Teams A and B should alternate playing parts.

<u>In Practice—Wednesday Morning 9:30 A.M.</u>
Quick Focus Warm-Up—15 to 45 seconds
Sound Activity—Dividing the Class into Groups

Divide the group into three teams: A, B, and C.
Slowly count 1, 2, 3, 1, 2, 3, etc. Team A plays a flat clap on 1.
Team B plays a back-and-forth rub on 2.
Team C stomps on 3.
Switch parts among the teams.

<u>In Practice—Wednesday 12 Noon</u>
Quick Focus Warm-Up—15 to 45 seconds
Sound Activity—Dividing the Class into Groups

Divide the group into three teams: A, B, and C.
Slowly count 1, 2, 3, 1, 2, 3, etc. Team A plays a flat clap on 1.
Team B plays a back-and-forth rub on 2.
Team C stomps on 3.
Switch parts among the teams.

In Practice—Wednesday 2 P.M.
Quick Focus Warm-Up—15 to 45 seconds
Sound Activity—Dividing the Class into Groups

Divide the group into three teams: A, B, and C.
    Slowly count 1, 2, 3, 1, 2, 3, etc. Team A plays a flat clap on 1.
    Team B plays a back-and-forth rub on 2.
    Team C stomps on 3.
    Switch parts among the teams

In Practice—Thursday Morning 9:30 A.M.
Quick Focus Warm-Up—15 to 45 seconds
Sound Activity—Dividing the Class into Groups

Divide the group into two teams: A and B.
    Now, pass one clap between the teams, similar to passing a clap one-to-one.

In Practice—Thursday 12 Noon
Quick Focus Warm-Up—15 to 45 seconds
Sound Activity—Dividing the Class into Groups

Divide the group into two teams: A and B.
    Now, pass one clap between the teams, similar to passing a clap one-to-one.

In Practice—Thursday 2 P.M.
Quick Focus Warm-Up—15 to 45 seconds
Sound Activity—Dividing the Class into Groups

Divide the group into two teams: A and B.
    Now, pass one clap between the teams, similar to passing a clap one-to-one.

In Practice—Friday Morning 9:30 A.M.
Quick Focus Warm-Up—15 to 45 seconds
Sound Activity—Dividing the Class into Groups

Have the class decide what to do.

> In Practice—Friday 12 Noon
> Quick Focus Warm-Up—15 to 45 seconds
> Sound Activity—Dividing the Class into Groups

Have the class decide what to do.

> In Practice—Friday 2 P.M.
> Quick Focus Warm-Up—15 to 45 seconds
> Sound Activity—Dividing the Class into Groups

Have the class decide what to do.

Week 8—Improvising and Creating Dialogue

This is about creating a conversation with abstract sounds in which two or more people actively participate, much like a conversation with words, but now with abstract sounds.

Please note to make sure your students incorporate all of the different types of Sound Activities we have learned so far. Everything that we have learned and worked with should be included in these conversations.

> In Practice—Monday 9:30 A.M.
> Quick Focus Warm-Up—15 to 45 seconds
> Sound Activity—Improvising and Creating Dialogue

To begin, divide your class into pairs, similar to passing a clap one-to-one.

Have one student play a short sound idea to their partner.

Then the partner must reply, first by repeating that sound idea and then by making a new one up of their own.

Repeat this process several times—repeat, then make up new; repeat, then make up new.

> In Practice—Monday 12 Noon
> Quick Focus Warm-Up—15 to 45 seconds
> Sound Activity—Improvising and Creating Dialogue

To begin, divide your class into pairs, similar to passing a clap one-to-one.

Have one student play a short sound idea to their partner.

Then the partner must reply, first by repeating that sound idea and then by making a new one up of their own.

Repeat this process several times—repeat, then make up new; repeat, then make up new.

<u>In Practice—Monday 2 P.M.</u>
Quick Focus Warm-Up—15 to 45 seconds
Sound Activity—Improvising and Creating Dialogue

To begin, divide your class into pairs, similar to passing a clap one-to-one.

Have one student play a short sound idea to their partner.

Then the partner must reply, first by repeating that sound idea and then by making a new one up of their own.

Repeat this process several times—repeat, then make up new; repeat, then make up new.

<u>In Practice—Tuesday Morning 9:30 A.M.</u>
Quick Focus Warm-Up—15 to 45 seconds
Sound Activity—Improvising and Creating Dialogue

To begin, divide your class into pairs, similar to passing a clap one-to-one.

Have one student play a short sound idea to their partner.

Then the partner must reply, first by repeating that sound idea and then by making a new one up of their own.

Repeat this process several times—repeat, then make up new; repeat, then make up new.

<u>In Practice—Tuesday 12 Noon</u>
Quick Focus Warm-Up—15 to 45 seconds
Sound Activity—Improvising and Creating Dialogue

To begin, divide your class into pairs, similar to passing a clap one-to-one.

Have one student play a short sound idea to their partner.

Then the partner must reply, first by repeating that sound idea and then by making a new one up of their own.

Repeat this process several times—repeat, then make up new; repeat, then make up new.

In Practice—Tuesday 2 P.M.
Quick Focus Warm-Up—15 to 45 seconds
Sound Activity—Improvising and Creating Dialogue

To begin, divide your class into pairs, similar to passing a clap one-to-one.

Have one student play a short sound idea to their partner.

Then the partner must reply, first by repeating that sound idea and then by making a new one up of their own.

Repeat this process several times—repeat, then make up new; repeat, then make up new.

In Practice—Wednesday Morning 9:30 A.M.
Quick Focus Warm-Up—15 to 45 seconds
Sound Activity—Improvising and Creating Dialogue

Enlarge the groups to three students.

Have one student play a short sound idea to their partner.

Then the partner must reply, first by repeating that sound idea and then by making a new one up of their own.

Repeat this process several times—repeat, then make up new; repeat, then make up new.

In Practice—Wednesday 12 Noon
Quick Focus Warm-Up—15 to 45 seconds
Sound Activity—Improvising and Creating Dialogue

Enlarge the groups to three students.

Have one student play a short sound idea to their partner.

Then the partner must reply, first by repeating that sound idea, and then by making a new one up of their own.

Repeat this process several times—repeat, then make up new; repeat, then make up new.

In Practice—Wednesday 2 P.M.
Quick Focus Warm-Up—15 to 45 seconds
Sound Activity—Improvising and Creating Dialogue

Enlarge the groups to three students.
Have one student play a short sound idea to their partner.
Then the partner must reply, first by repeating that sound idea, and then by making a new one up of their own.
Repeat this process several times—repeat, then make up new; repeat, then make up new.

In Practice—Thursday Morning 9:30 A.M.
Quick Focus Warm-Up—15 to 45 seconds
Sound Activity—Improvising and Creating Dialogue

Pair your students up in twos.
Remove all instructions and encourage your students to just improvise and respond to each other in the moment.
They are free to take turns or not as they see fit but, most importantly, always listen to their partner.

In Practice—Thursday 12 Noon
Quick Focus Warm-Up—15 to 45 seconds
Sound Activity—Improvising and Creating Dialogue

Pair your students up in twos.
Remove all instructions and encourage your students to just improvise and respond to each other in the moment.
They are free to take turns or not as they see fit but, most importantly, always listen to their partner.

In Practice—Thursday 2 P.M.
Quick Focus Warm-Up—15 to 45 seconds
Sound Activity—Improvising and Creating Dialogue

Pair your students up in twos.

Remove all instructions and encourage your students to just improvise and respond to each other in the moment.

They are free to take turns or not as they see fit but, most importantly, always listen to their partner.

<u>In Practice—Friday Morning 9:30 A.M.</u>
Quick Focus Warm-Up—15 to 45 seconds
Sound Activity—Improvising and Creating Dialogue

Pair your students up in twos.

Remove all instructions and encourage your students to just improvise and respond to each other in the moment.

They are free to take turns or not as they see fit but, most importantly, always listen to their partner.

<u>In Practice—Friday 12 Noon</u>
Quick Focus Warm-Up—15 to 45 seconds
Sound Activity—Improvising and Creating Dialogue

Pair your students up in twos.

Remove all instructions and encourage your students to just improvise and respond to each other in the moment.

They are free to take turns or not as they see fit but, most importantly, always listen to their partner.

<u>In Practice—Friday 2 P.M.</u>
Quick Focus Warm-Up—15 to 45 seconds
Sound Activity—Improvising and Creating Dialogue

Pair your students up in twos.

Remove all instructions and encourage your students to just improvise and respond to each other in the moment.

They are free to take turns or not as they see fit but, most importantly, always listen to their partner.

Week 9—Rhythmic Literacy

This is applying two basic traditional music notation symbols to actively make sound and silence: a quarter note, which is the equivalent of one beat of sound, and a quarter-note rest, which is the equivalent of one beat of rest or silence.

It is imperative to understand that playing silence is as important, if not more important, than playing sound. Creating silence is a deliberate task that gives shape and importance to all sounds.

Above is the symbol for a quarter note, which equals one beat of sound.

Above is the symbol for a quarter rest, which equals one beat of silence (no sound).

<u>In Practice—Monday 9:30 A.M.</u>
Quick Focus Warm-Up—15 to 45 seconds
Sound Activity—Rhythmic Literacy

Draw this exercise on your board and have your students count out loud and play a flat clap for every note and beat.

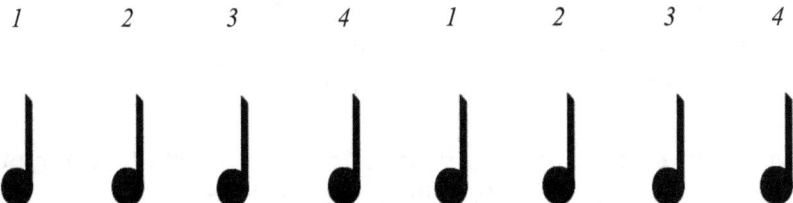

In Practice—Monday 12 Noon
Quick Focus Warm-Up—15 to 45 seconds
Sound Activity—Rhythmic Literacy

Draw this exercise on your board and have your students count out loud and play a rest or beat of silence for every beat they count. Your students are to actively play silence.

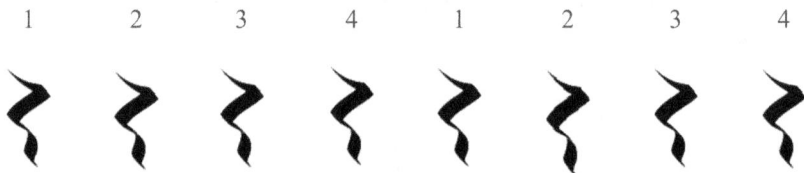

In Practice—Monday 2 P.M.
Quick Focus Warm-Up—15 to 45 seconds
Sound Activity—Rhythmic Literacy

Draw this exercise on your board and have your students count out loud and play a flat clap when they see the quarter-note symbol, which indicates a sound should be made, and play a beat of silence for when they see a rest symbol.

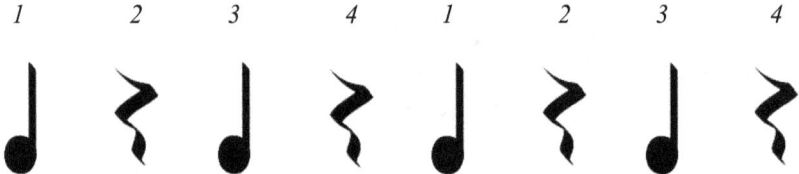

In Practice—Tuesday Morning 9:30 A.M.
Quick Focus Warm-Up—15 to 45 seconds
Sound Activity—Rhythmic Literacy

Draw this exercise on your board and have your students count out loud and play a flat clap when they see the quarter-note symbol indicating sound, and play a beat of silence for when they see a rest symbol.

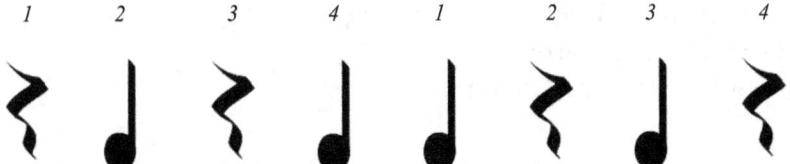

<u>In Practice—Tuesday 12 Noon</u>
Quick Focus Warm-Up—15 to 45 seconds
Sound Activity—Rhythmic Literacy

Draw this exercise on your board and have your students count out loud and play a flat clap when they see the quarter-note symbol indicating sound, and play a beat of silence for when they see a rest symbol.

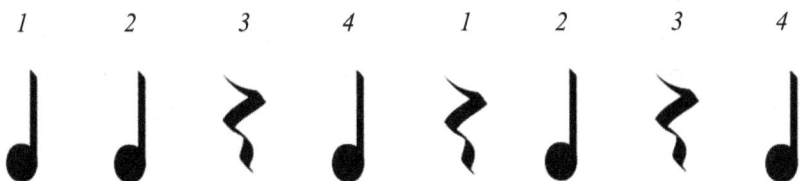

<u>In Practice—Tuesday 2 P.M.</u>
Quick Focus Warm-Up—15 to 45 seconds
Sound Activity—Rhythmic Literacy

Draw this exercise on your board and have your students count out loud and play a flat clap when they see the quarter-note symbol indicating sound, and play a beat of silence for when they see a rest symbol.

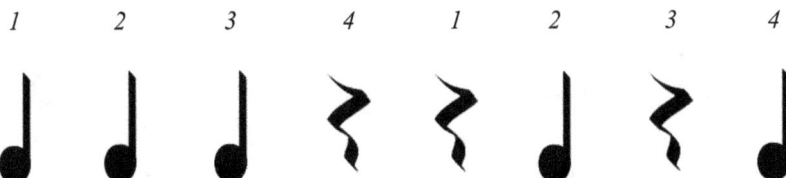

In Practice—Wednesday Morning 9:30 A.M.
Quick Focus Warm-Up—15 to 45 seconds
Sound Activity—Rhythmic Literacy

Draw this exercise on your board and have your students count out loud and play a flat clap when they see the quarter-note symbol indicating sound, and play a beat of silence for when they see a rest symbol.

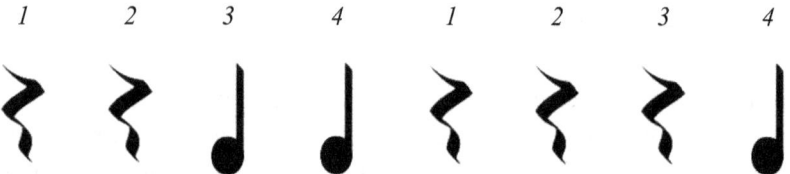

Adding Complexity

Now that everyone is comfortable with clapping, let's add a stomp into the mix. To do this, simply turn the quarter-note symbol upside down. This becomes the visual symbol of a quarter-note stomp.

This is the symbol for a quarter-note clap.

This is the symbol for a quarter-note stomp.

This is the symbol for a quarter-note rest or a beat of silence.

In Practice—Wednesday 12 Noon
Quick Focus Warm-Up—15 to 45 seconds
Sound Activity—Rhythmic Literacy

Draw this exercise on your board and have your students count out loud and play a flat clap, a stomp, and a beat of silence when they read the appropriate symbol.

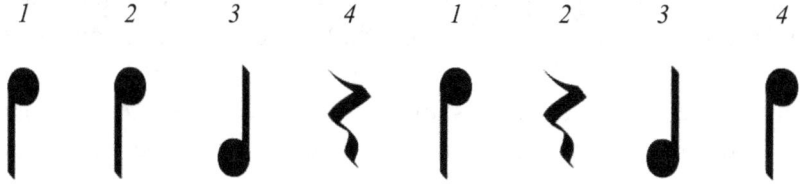

In Practice—Wednesday 2 P.M.
Quick Focus Warm-Up—15 to 45 seconds
Sound Activity—Rhythmic Literacy

Draw this exercise on your board and have your students count out loud and play a flat clap, a stomp, and a beat of silence when they read the appropriate symbol.

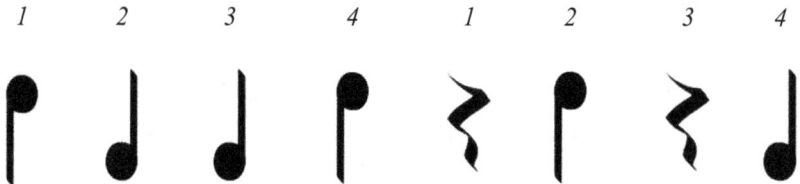

In Practice—Thursday Morning 9:30 A.M.
Quick Focus Warm-Up—15 to 45 seconds
Sound Activity—Rhythmic Literacy

Draw this exercise on your board and have your students count out loud and play a flat clap, a stomp, and a beat of silence when they read the appropriate symbol.

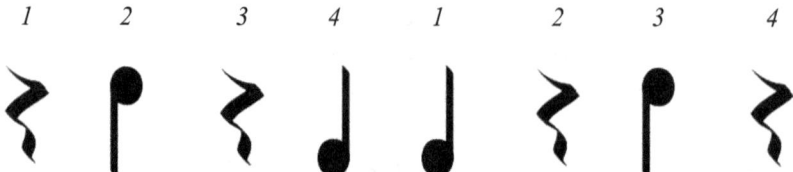

Adding in Even a Little More Additional Complexity

Let's not forget about what Cecilia's class decided. Her 3-year-olds simply applied color as a way to make quarter notes even more dynamic and decided that because red, yellow, and orange are hot colors, quarter-note symbols in those colors should be played as loud sounds. While quarter-note symbols in blue, purple, and green—the cool colors—may be played as quiet sounds.

In Practice—Thursday 12 Noon
Quick Focus Warm-Up—15 to 45 seconds
Sound Activity—Rhythmic Literacy

Draw this exercise on your board and have your students count out loud and play a flat clap, a stomp, and a beat of silence when they read the appropriate symbol.

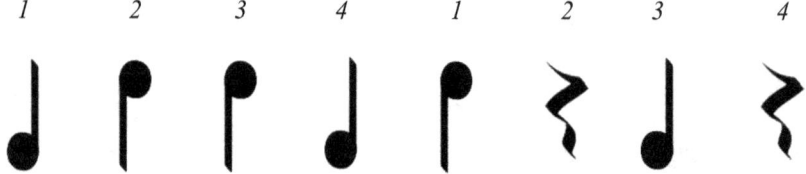

In Practice—Thursday 2 P.M.
Quick Focus Warm-Up—15 to 45 seconds
Sound Activity—Rhythmic Literacy

Draw this exercise on your board and have your students count out loud and play a flat clap, a stomp, and a beat of silence when they read the appropriate symbol.

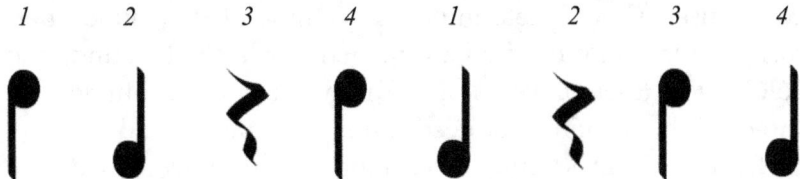

In Practice—Friday Morning 9:30 A.M.
Quick Focus Warm-Up—15 to 45 seconds
Sound Activity—Rhythmic Literacy

Invite a student to draw and lead a counting, clapping, stomping, and resting.

In Practice—Friday 12 Noon
Quick Focus Warm-Up—15 to 45 seconds
Sound Activity—Rhythmic Literacy

Invite a student to draw and lead a counting, clapping, stomping, and resting.

In Practice—Friday 2 P.M.
Quick Focus Warm-Up—15 to 45 seconds
Sound Activity—Rhythmic Literacy

Invite a student to draw and lead a counting, clapping, stomping, and resting.

Week 10—Art Sounds

Art Sounds is simply using your students' artwork—drawings, paintings, collages, papier-mâché, constructions, assemblages, or sculptures—as a prompt to organize, interpret, compose, and perform sound. I have tried this many times and believe me, it is one of the most fun and free Creative Sound Play exercises. For the most part, it should be left up to the children to decide how the artwork will sound, but as always it is helpful to offer some guidelines. One teacher suggested that the number of colors used should determine the volume of the sounds performed. One color equaled a quiet (soft or hushed) sound, two colors were to be played at a medium or ordinary volume, and three colors or more produced loud, exuberant sounds (Figure 14.1, see p. 67). In addition to teaching students how to modulate their sound and expression, this encourages visual discrimination, leading students to look at their art in a whole new way and how they may want to tell a story.

By pointing at or holding up a painting for 10 or so seconds, in any order, a child can have their paintings performed by the ensemble (class).

But why stop at color as a prompt when there is so much more in art that can inspire thoughtful, meaningful sound? What if anything is being depicted? What are the different colors? How was the paint applied? Are the marks round or straight, short or long? These are all elements that can be used as prompts to help students create a host of fun, deliberate, and intentional sounds. Let's examine these three finger paintings to see what I mean.

First, take the blue painting, which was sounded as "Quiet" because it had only one color. But what about paint application? Don't those round swirls suggest the quiet sound that comes from rubbing hands together in a circular motion, as we learned earlier in the Technique and Texture Sound Activity? This painting could also inspire quiet, repeated vocal sounds, for example running words together to create a "spinning" sound: Wish-You, Wish-You, Wish-You etc. This can be a lot of fun, especially when you start playing around with the speed or tempo by slowing down or speeding up the Wish-You, Wish-You, Wish-You, or You-Wish, You-Wish, You-Wish. Once the students are making theses sounds, try having them close their eyes to let go of the visual prompt and experience just hearing the sound itself as a texture filling the room.

The middle painting was sounded at "Medium" volume because it used two colors, blue and magenta. Another way to approach such a painting would be to divide your class in two (or let them choose) and have each half sound one of the colors. Then have the two groups take turns, passing their sounds back and forth, at first simply and then with overlaps—the sound for blue begins, then lingers and slowly diminishes as the magenta sound enters and takes center stage, lingers, and then fades away in turn as the sound for blue begins a new cycle. Plus, since the finger marks in both the blue and magenta colors resemble a variety of different lengths of strokes, so should the durations of the all the sounds. This will also call everyone's attention to what happens at the important part of the painting where the two colors meet. And needless to say, this exercise would provide a wonderful opportunity for students to conduct the class.

Finally, the painting on the right was sounded as "Loud" because it had three or more colors. But look: it also consists of oval type, multi-colored dots with space or "Silence" between them. This punctuated structure makes it perfect for the four types of claps we've already learned: flat, monster, applause, and pat claps. After going over the four types, have each student clap once and then stop, wait, and create space by playing silence before they clap again. The element of chance in this group activity will be lots of fun as the claps bump into each other or try to stay out of each other's way. Then, to add complexity to the sound palette, offer your students stomps and short vocal sounds as well.

In addition to these whole-class activities, try dividing your class into groups and assign each group a different painting to sound out. Let the groups know that after discussing and coming up with their own approach, they will be able to share it with the class and get feedback. And for variety or to extend the activity, switch up the groups and paintings.

Of course, there are many other factors that can be brought into consideration: shapes and directions of lines, their thicknesses, the density of images, the areas of the artwork left untouched or blank, and the kinds of materials used, such as colored paper, tissue paper, crayons, paint, pencils, tape, string, buttons, cork, bottle caps, sparkles, etc. All of these can and do suggest sound. You can use artworks that have already been made or ask your students to make art knowing that it will become part of a sound piece. And don't forget, just as a piece of music can have different sections or movements, a sound piece can be triggered by one artwork or several, it's all up to the child.

> In Practice—Monday through Friday 9:30 A.M., 12 Noon, and 2 P.M.
> Quick Focus Warm-Up—15 to 45 seconds
> Sound Activity—Art Sounds

Invite a student(s) to draw a picture(s) on the board, and have them explain how they want it to sound and then conduct their peers in sounding it out.

Week 11—Conducting through Patterns

This is using arms and hands to physically indicate one of three patterns for counting: **A, B,** or **C**.

> A–Counting 1, 2, 1, 2, 1, 2, etc.
> B–Counting 1, 2, 3, 1, 2, 3, 1, 2, 3, etc.
> C–Counting 1, 2, 3, 4, 1, 2, 3, 4, 1, 2, 3, 4, etc.

As you can see, each one of these patterns is determined by the number of beats:

> Pattern A—2 beats 1, 2
> Pattern B—3 beats 1, 2, 3
> Pattern C—4 beats 1, 2, 3, 4

Regardless of the number of beats in a pattern, the tempo is determined by the conductor through their gesture.

The first pattern is for counting 1, 2, 1, 2, 1, 2—regardless of the tempo—the hand pattern must resemble this (see the following). When one is saying the number 1, their hand or arm is moving in a downward motion, and when they say the number 2, it is moving upward.

The Weekly Schedule for Learning the 12 Sound Activities ♦ 143

In Practice—Monday 9:30 A.M.
Quick Focus Warm-Up—15 to 45 seconds
Sound Activity—Conducting through Patterns

Conducting Pattern A—2 beats
   Slowly count 1, 2, 1, 2, 1, 2, 1, 2, 1, 2, 1, 2, 1, 2, 1, 2, and so on.
   Use your right hand to conduct Pattern A.

In Practice—Monday 12 Noon
Quick Focus Warm-Up—15 to 45 seconds
Sound Activity—Conducting through Patterns

Conducting Pattern A—2 beats
   Slowly count 1, 2, 1, 2, 1, 2, 1, 2, 1, 2, 1, 2, 1, 2, 1, 2, and so on.
   Use your right hand to conduct Pattern A.

In Practice—Monday 2 P.M.
Quick Focus Warm-Up—15 to 45 seconds
Sound Activity—Conducting through Patterns

Conducting Pattern A—2 beats
   Slowly count 1, 2, 1, 2, 1, 2, 1, 2, 1, 2, 1, 2, 1, 2, 1, 2, and so on.
   Now, to add complexity, switch hands and use your left hand to conduct Pattern A.

In Practice—Tuesday Morning 9:30 A.M.
With Pattern B, the count is 1, 2, 3, 1, 2, 3, 2, 1, 2, 3—regardless of the tempo—the hand pattern must resemble this (see the following). The image for this is a triangle. For number 1,

the hand or arm moves in a downward motion. For number 2, the hand/arm moves horizontally outward to the left or right. For number 3, the hand/arm moves upward in a diagonal direction to where it first began, closing the triangle.

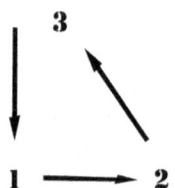

In Practice—Tuesday Morning 9:30 A.M.
Quick Focus Warm-Up—15 to 45 seconds
Sound Activity—Conducting through Patterns

Conducting Pattern B—3 beats
   Slowly count 1, 2, 3, 1, 2, 3, 2, 1, 2, 3, and so on.
   Use your right hand to conduct Pattern B.

In Practice—Tuesday 12 Noon
Quick Focus Warm-Up—15 to 45 seconds
Sound Activity—Conducting through Patterns

Conducting Pattern B—3 beats
   Slowly count 1, 2, 3, 1, 2, 3, 2, 1, 2, 3, and so on.
   Use your right hand to conduct Pattern B.

In Practice—Tuesday 2 P.M.
Quick Focus Warm-Up—15 to 45 seconds
Sound Activity—Conducting through Patterns

Conducting Pattern B—3 beats
   Slowly count is 1, 2, 3, 1, 2, 3, 2, 1, 2, 3, and so on.
   Now, to add complexity, switch hands and use your left hand to conduct Pattern B.

In Practice—Wednesday Morning 9:30 A.M.
With Pattern C, the counting is 1, 2, 3, 4, 1, 2, 3, 4, 1, 2, 3, 4, 1, 2, 3, 4.

The image for this is the outer points of a simple cross.

A simple cross	A cross with the beats
+	+ (4 top, 1 bottom, 2 left, 3 right)

Count out loud 1, 2, 3, 4, 1, 2, 3, 4, 1, 2, 3, 4, 1, 2, 3, 4, and so on.

As you count number 1, move your hand/arm downward. For number 2, move your hand upward in a diagonal direction to the left. Count the number 3 by moving your hand/arm horizontally across to the right. Complete the pattern by counting the number 4 and moving your hand/arm upward in a diagonal direction to where you began.

The conducting pattern looks like this.

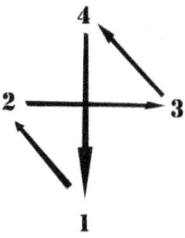

Think of the number 4 as your head, the number 1 as your belly button, the number 2 as your left shoulder, the number 3 as your right shoulder.

In Practice—Wednesday Morning 9:30 A.M.
Quick Focus Warm-Up—15 to 45 seconds
Sound Activity—Conducting through Patterns

Conducting Pattern C—4 beats
   Slowly count 1, 2, 3, 4, 1, 2, 3, 4, 1, 2, 3, 4, 1, 2, 3, 4, and so on.
   Use your right hand to conduct Pattern C.

   In Practice—Wednesday 12 Noon
   Quick Focus Warm-Up—15 to 45 seconds
   Sound Activity—Conducting through Patterns

Conducting Pattern C—4 beats
   Slowly count 1, 2, 3, 4, 1, 2, 3, 4, 1, 2, 3, 4, 1, 2, 3, 4. and so on.
   Use your right hand to conduct Pattern C.

   In Practice—Wednesday 2 P.M.
   Quick Focus Warm-Up—15 to 45 seconds
   Sound Activity—Conducting through Patterns

Conducting Pattern C—4 beats
   Slowly count 1, 2, 3, 4, 1, 2, 3, 4, 1, 2, 3, 4, 1, 2, 3, 4 and so on.
   Now, to add complexity, switch hands and use your left hand to conduct Pattern C

   In Practice—Thursday Morning 9:30 A.M.
   Quick Focus Warm-Up—15 to 45 seconds
   Sound Activity—Conducting through Patterns

Conducting Pattern C—4 beats
   Count slowly 1, 2, 3, 4, 1, 2, 3, 4, 1, 2, 3, 4, etc. Conduct Pattern C alternating between right and left arms and then together.

   In Practice—Thursday 12 Noon
   Quick Focus Warm-Up—15 to 45 seconds
   Sound Activity—Conducting through Patterns

Conducting Pattern B—3 beats
   Count slowly 1, 2, 3, 1, 2, 3, 2, 1, 2, 3, etc.
   Conduct Pattern B alternating between right and left arms and then together.

In Practice—Thursday 2 P.M.
Quick Focus Warm-Up—15 to 45 seconds
Sound Activity—Conducting through Patterns

Conducting Pattern A—2 beats
　　Count slowly 1, 2, 1, 2, 1, 2, 1, 2, 1, 2, 1, 2, 1, 2, 1, 2, and so on.
　　Conduct Pattern A alternating between right and left arms and then together.

In Practice—Friday Morning 9:30 A.M.
Quick Focus Warm-Up—15 to 45 seconds
Sound Activity—Conducting through Patterns

Invite students to decide on what kind of gesture they want to use to conduct and lead the class.

In Practice—Friday 12 Noon
Quick Focus Warm-Up—15 to 45 seconds
Sound Activity—Conducting through Patterns

Invite students to decide on what kind of gesture they want to use to conduct and lead the class.

In Practice—Friday 2 P.M.
Quick Focus Warm-Up—15 to 45 seconds
Sound Activity—Conducting through Patterns

Invite students to decide on what kind of gesture they want to use to conduct and lead the class.

Week 12—Conducting through Gesture
This is freely using any kind of physical gesture to indicate where sound begins and ends, it's volume(s), how dense, who plays it at any given time, etc.

In Practice—Monday through Friday 9:30 A.M., 12 Noon, and 2 P.M.
Quick Focus Warm-Up—15 to 45 seconds
Sound Activity—Conducting through Gesture

Invite a different student to conduct the class strictly through gesture without any verbal instructions.

Week 13—Review

<u>In Practice—Monday 9:30 A.M.</u>
Quick Focus Warm-Up—15 to 45 seconds
Sound Activity—Counting, Clapping, and Stomping

Counting out loud 1, 2, 3, 4, 1, 2, 3, 4, 1, 2, 3, 4, etc.
Monster clap on 1, left foot stomp on 2, silence on 3, circular rub on 4.

<u>In Practice—Monday 12 Noon</u>
Quick Focus Warm-Up—15 to 45 seconds
Sound Activity—Counting, Clapping and Stomping

Counting out loud 1, 2, 3, 4, 1, 2, 3, 4, 1, 2, 3, 4, etc.
Pat clap on 1, silence on 2, bark on 3, circular rub on 4

<u>In Practice—Monday 2 P.M.</u>
Quick Focus Warm-Up—15 to 45 seconds
Sound Activity—Technique and Texture

Have students demonstrate and lead the four different types of ways to clap and the two ways to rub hands.

<u>In Practice—Tuesday Morning 9:30 A.M.</u>
Quick Focus Warm-Up—15 to 45 seconds
Sound Activity—Technique and Texture

Have students demonstrate and lead the four different types of ways to clap and the two ways to rub hands.

<u>In Practice—Tuesday 12 Noon</u>
Quick Focus Warm-Up—15 to 45 seconds
Sound Activity—Dynamic Control

Count 1, 2, 3, 1, 2, 3, 1, 2, 3.

Play every beat with an applause clap. Start very softly and gradually get louder and louder. This exercise should take at least 20 to 30 seconds to go from the softest clap to the loudest clap.

Count 1, 2, 3, 4, 1, 2, 3, 4. Play every beat with an applause clap; start very loudly and gradually get softer and softer. This exercise should take at least 20 to 30 seconds to go from the loudest clap to the softest clap.

Play three different levels of volume: softly (pianissimo), medium (mezzo forte), and loudly (forte).

<u>In Practice—Tuesday 2 P.M.</u>
Quick Focus Warm-Up—15 to 45 seconds
Sound Activity—Dynamic Control

Count 1, 2, 3, 1, 2, 3, 1, 2, 3. Play every beat with an applause clap. Start very softly and gradually get louder and louder. This exercise should take at least 20 to 30 seconds to go from the softest clap to the loudest clap.

Count 1, 2, 3, 4, 1, 2, 3, 4. Play every beat with an applause clap. Start very loudly and gradually get softer and softer. This exercise should take at least 20 to 30 seconds to go from the loudest clap to the softest clap.

Play three different levels of volume: softly (pianissimo), medium (mezzo forte), and loudly (forte).

<u>In Practice—Wednesday Morning 9:30 A.M.</u>
Quick Focus Warm-Up—15 to 45 seconds
Sound Activity—Emphasis, Duration and Pitch

Slowly count out loud in a whisper 1, 2, 3, 4, 1, 2, 3, 4, etc. Play everything short.

Whisper short on 1; high vocal sound, loud, and long on 2; stomp on 3; and do a flat clap on 4.

<u>In Practice—Wednesday 12 Noon</u>
Quick Focus Warm-Up—15 to 45 seconds
Sound Activity—Emphasis, Duration, and Pitch

Slowly count out loud in a whisper 1, 2, 3, 4, 1, 2, 3, 4, etc. Play everything short.

Whisper short on 1; high vocal sound, loud, and long on 2; stomp on 3; and do a flat clap on 4.

In Practice—Wednesday 2 P.M.
Quick Focus Warm-Up—15 to 45 seconds
Sound Activity—Time and Tempo

Have your students close their eyes, listen to you, and clap with you. Start slowly and quietly. After at least 10 seconds at a constant slow tempo, gradually get faster, but make sure the volume doesn't get louder. When you reach a fast tempo, keep it constant for at least 10 seconds, then gradually slow down to where you began. Make sure everyone maintains a steady volume throughout the whole exercise. The volume will most likely get louder as you speed up and get softer as you slow down, but try to prevent that from happening.

In Practice—Thursday Morning 9:30 A.M.
Quick Focus Warm-Up—15 to 45 seconds
Sound Activity—Passing a Clap One-to-One

Have the class stand or sit in a full circle. Count off a moderate tempo and pass the clap around the room. Change directions.

In Practice—Thursday 12 Noon
Quick Focus Warm-Up—15 to 45 seconds
Sound Activity—Dividing the Class into Groups

Divide the group into three teams: A, B, and C.
    Slowly count 1, 2, 3, 1, 2, 3, etc.
    Team A is to play a flat clap on 1.
    Team B is to play a back-and-forth rub on 2.
    Team C is to stomp on 3.

In Practice—Thursday 2 P.M.
Quick Focus Warm-Up—15 to 45 seconds
Sound Activity—Improvising and Creating Dialogue

Make sure your students incorporate different types of sounds, textures, and volumes. Everything we have learned and worked with related to sound should be included in these conversations.

Make groups of three students.

Have one student play a sound idea to their partner.

The partner must repeat it back to them and then turn to the third (new) student and create a new sound idea that is different and of their own creation.

This student must repeat it back to them and then create something new and different that is of their own creation and pass that on to the next student.

Repeat several times.

In Practice—Friday Morning 9:30 A.M.
Quick Focus Warm-Up—15 to 45 seconds
Sound Activity—Improvising and Creating Dialogue

Arrange your students in groups of three.

Let them express themselves however they want, free of having to have to play back what the other partner said or played.

Try to get them to really listen to each other and respond to each other in the moment, just like a conversation one might have with a friend, but instead of using words, use abstract sounds.

In Practice—Friday 12 Noon
Quick Focus Warm-Up—15 to 45 seconds
Sound Activity—Rhythmic Literacy

Draw this exercise on your board. Have your students count out loud and play a flat clap, a stomp, and a beat of silence when they read the appropriate symbol.

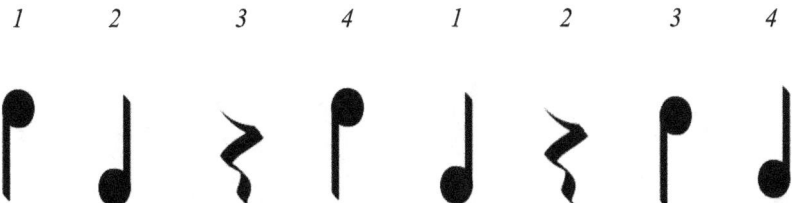

In Practice—Friday 2 P.M.
Quick Focus Warm-Up—15 to 45 seconds
Sound Activity—Conducting through Patterns

A 4 Pattern. Count slowly out loud 1, 2, 3, 4, 1, 2, 3, 4, 1, 2, 3, 4, etc. Conduct the 4 pattern by alternating between right hand, left hand, and hands and arms together.

Sound Activity—Conducting through Gesture

Instead of using gestures that outline a pattern, freely conduct to prompt your students to make whatever sounds they feel like making. Move your hand(s) up to make the students get louder and down to make them softer. Wiggle your fingers or shake your hands to have them make faster sounds.

Afterword

One of the things I love about Creative Sound Play is that it uses something as simple as sound, which is ever present and doesn't need anything expensive to do. All we need are our bodies to make sound; yet it's so rich and filled with so many possibilities, like all the kinds of variations we can make. There are variations in volume, pitch, and duration; there's variation in intensity, tempo, and timing; there's variation by mood and something people don't usually think about, there's variation in absence and presents, there's silence. So out of something so simple there's a world of possibilities, infinite possibilities.

It also creates the feeling of community and the feeling that we all belong—that as a part of the community we learn to cooperate, we learn to collaborate, we learn to play off one and other, and to take turns. We learn that together we can make something that can be even better then what we might do on our own, and that each one of us is needed, is an important contributor, and if we take one of us out we lose part of the beauty of the sound we can make together as a group.

Creative Sound Play is as open to the poor kid as it is to the rich kid. It helps to support so many of the things that are critical for the best executive functions because it creates joy, helps to reduce stress, and builds community.

Adele Diamond, PhD, FRSC, Canada Research Chair Professor of Developmental Cognitive Neuroscience, Head of Program in Developmental Cognitive Neuroscience, University of British Columbia, Vancouver

Reference Articles Regarding Executive Function

Diamond, A., & Lee, K. (2011). Interventions shown to aid executive function development in children 4 to 12 years old. *Science*, 333 (6045), 959–964.

Ursache, A., Blair, C., & Raver, C.C. (2012). The promotion of self-regulation as a means of enhancing school readiness and early achievement in children at risk for school failure. *Child Development Perspectives*, 6, 122–128.

Blair, C. & Raver, C.C. (2015). School readiness and self-regulation: A developmental psychobiological approach. *Annual Review of Psychology*, 66, 711–731.

Moreno, S., & Lee, Y. (2015). Short-term second language and music training induces lasting functional brain changes in early childhood. *Child Development*, 86 (2), 394–406.

Bibliography

Galinsky, Ellen. *Mind in the Making: The Seven Essential Life Skills Every Child Needs*. New York: HarperCollins, 2010.

Golinkoff, Roberta Michnick and Kathy Hirsh-Pasek. *Becoming Briliant: What Science Tells Us About Raising Successful Children*. Washington, DC: American Psychological Association Life Tools, 2016.

Kraus, Nina. *Of Sound Mind, How Our Brain Constructs a Meaningful Sonic World*. Cambridge, MA: MIT Press, 2021.

Magsamen, Susan and Ivy Ross. *Your Brain on Art*. New York: Random House, 2023.

Nathan, Linda. *When Grit Is Not Enough: A High School Principal Examines How Poverty and Inequality Thwart the College-For-All Promise*. Boston: Beacon Press, 2017.